The Book Of

Indomitable Virtues

Clay Roueche

THE BOOK OF INDOMITABLE VIRTUES

Self-Published with assistance from

Midnight Express Books

POBox 69
Berryville AR 72616
(870) 210-3772
MEBooks1@yahoo.com

This book is dedicated to my parents, my daughters 'The Three C's', and to all those who still have faith in me under any circumstances.

Like the Japanese proverb says: 7 times down, 8 times up. I appreciate you all.

Love & Respect 888

Author's Family Crest

I BELIEVE, NO MATTER WHAT
A PERSON'S PAST MAY HAVE BEEN,
THEIR FUTURE IS
WHATEVER THEY CHOOSE
TO MAKE IT.

– CLAY ROUECHE

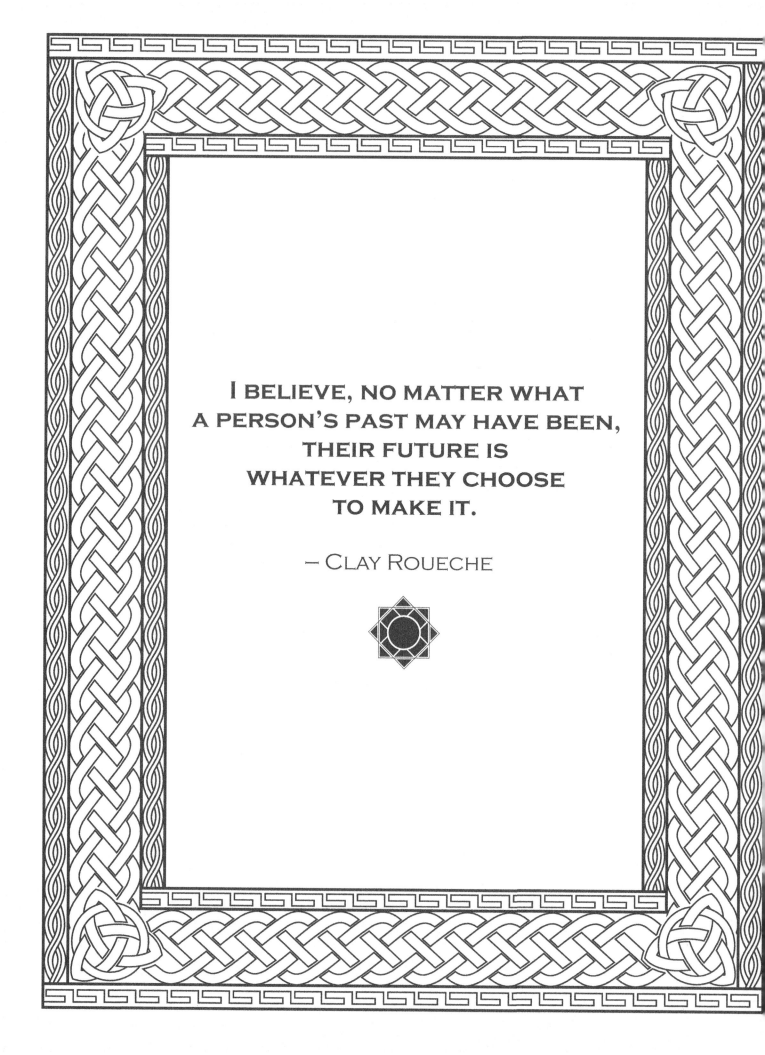

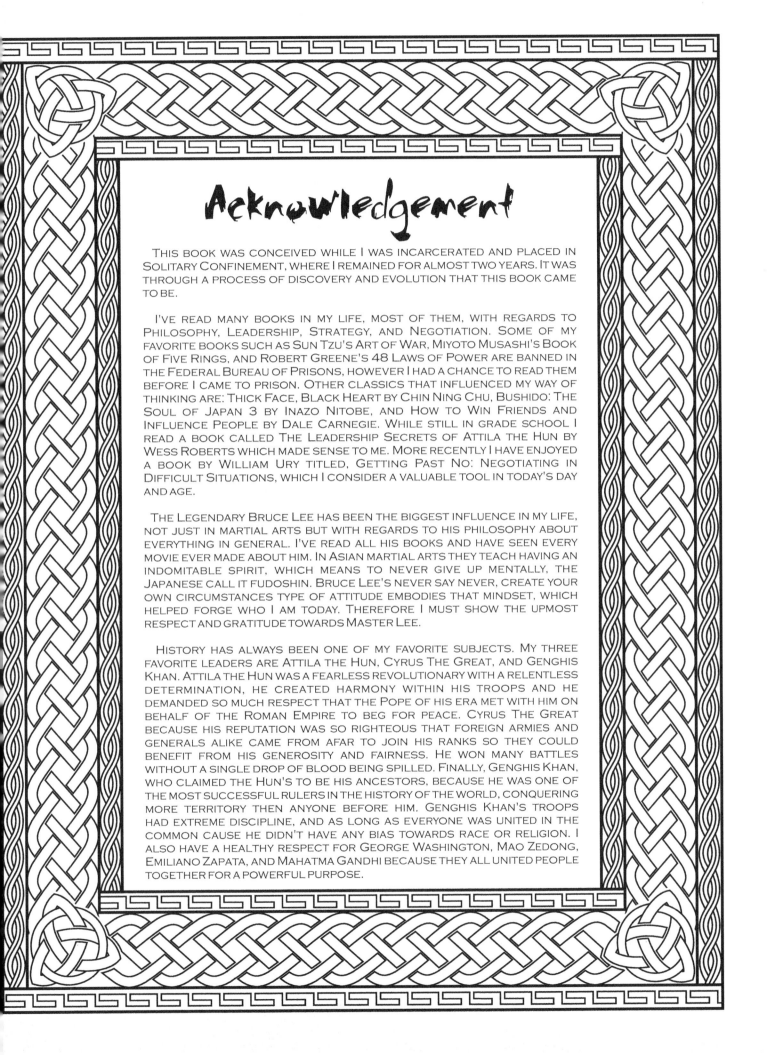

Acknowledgement

THIS BOOK WAS CONCEIVED WHILE I WAS INCARCERATED AND PLACED IN SOLITARY CONFINEMENT, WHERE I REMAINED FOR ALMOST TWO YEARS. IT WAS THROUGH A PROCESS OF DISCOVERY AND EVOLUTION THAT THIS BOOK CAME TO BE.

I'VE READ MANY BOOKS IN MY LIFE, MOST OF THEM, WITH REGARDS TO PHILOSOPHY, LEADERSHIP, STRATEGY, AND NEGOTIATION. SOME OF MY FAVORITE BOOKS SUCH AS SUN TZU'S ART OF WAR, MIYOTO MUSASHI'S BOOK OF FIVE RINGS, AND ROBERT GREENE'S 48 LAWS OF POWER ARE BANNED IN THE FEDERAL BUREAU OF PRISONS, HOWEVER I HAD A CHANCE TO READ THEM BEFORE I CAME TO PRISON. OTHER CLASSICS THAT INFLUENCED MY WAY OF THINKING ARE: THICK FACE, BLACK HEART BY CHIN NING CHU, BUSHIDO: THE SOUL OF JAPAN 3 BY INAZO NITOBE, AND HOW TO WIN FRIENDS AND INFLUENCE PEOPLE BY DALE CARNEGIE. WHILE STILL IN GRADE SCHOOL I READ A BOOK CALLED THE LEADERSHIP SECRETS OF ATTILA THE HUN BY WESS ROBERTS WHICH MADE SENSE TO ME. MORE RECENTLY I HAVE ENJOYED A BOOK BY WILLIAM URY TITLED, GETTING PAST NO: NEGOTIATING IN DIFFICULT SITUATIONS, WHICH I CONSIDER A VALUABLE TOOL IN TODAY'S DAY AND AGE.

THE LEGENDARY BRUCE LEE HAS BEEN THE BIGGEST INFLUENCE IN MY LIFE, NOT JUST IN MARTIAL ARTS BUT WITH REGARDS TO HIS PHILOSOPHY ABOUT EVERYTHING IN GENERAL. I'VE READ ALL HIS BOOKS AND HAVE SEEN EVERY MOVIE EVER MADE ABOUT HIM. IN ASIAN MARTIAL ARTS THEY TEACH HAVING AN INDOMITABLE SPIRIT, WHICH MEANS TO NEVER GIVE UP MENTALLY, THE JAPANESE CALL IT FUDOSHIN. BRUCE LEE'S NEVER SAY NEVER, CREATE YOUR OWN CIRCUMSTANCES TYPE OF ATTITUDE EMBODIES THAT MINDSET, WHICH HELPED FORGE WHO I AM TODAY. THEREFORE I MUST SHOW THE UPMOST RESPECT AND GRATITUDE TOWARDS MASTER LEE.

HISTORY HAS ALWAYS BEEN ONE OF MY FAVORITE SUBJECTS. MY THREE FAVORITE LEADERS ARE ATTILA THE HUN, CYRUS THE GREAT, AND GENGHIS KHAN. ATTILA THE HUN WAS A FEARLESS REVOLUTIONARY WITH A RELENTLESS DETERMINATION, HE CREATED HARMONY WITHIN HIS TROOPS AND HE DEMANDED SO MUCH RESPECT THAT THE POPE OF HIS ERA MET WITH HIM ON BEHALF OF THE ROMAN EMPIRE TO BEG FOR PEACE. CYRUS THE GREAT BECAUSE HIS REPUTATION WAS SO RIGHTEOUS THAT FOREIGN ARMIES AND GENERALS ALIKE CAME FROM AFAR TO JOIN HIS RANKS SO THEY COULD BENEFIT FROM HIS GENEROSITY AND FAIRNESS. HE WON MANY BATTLES WITHOUT A SINGLE DROP OF BLOOD BEING SPILLED. FINALLY, GENGHIS KHAN, WHO CLAIMED THE HUN'S TO BE HIS ANCESTORS, BECAUSE HE WAS ONE OF THE MOST SUCCESSFUL RULERS IN THE HISTORY OF THE WORLD, CONQUERING MORE TERRITORY THEN ANYONE BEFORE HIM. GENGHIS KHAN'S TROOPS HAD EXTREME DISCIPLINE, AND AS LONG AS EVERYONE WAS UNITED IN THE COMMON CAUSE HE DIDN'T HAVE ANY BIAS TOWARDS RACE OR RELIGION. I ALSO HAVE A HEALTHY RESPECT FOR GEORGE WASHINGTON, MAO ZEDONG, EMILIANO ZAPATA, AND MAHATMA GANDHI BECAUSE THEY ALL UNITED PEOPLE TOGETHER FOR A POWERFUL PURPOSE.

I HAVE ALWAYS FELT DRAWN TO THE ASIAN WAY OF THINKING, IT WAS A NATURAL FIT FOR ME. PERHAPS IT'S BECAUSE OF MY MOM'S MONGOLIAN DNA. STUDYING ASIAN MARTIAL ARTS SERVED AS MY GATEWAY INTO THE DIFFERENT SYSTEMS OF THOUGHT. I STUDIED BUDDHISM, DAOISM, SHINTOISM, AND CONFUCIANISM. THERE IS MANY DIFFERENT TYPES OF SPELLINGS FOR CHINESE WORDS IN ENGLISH, TO KEEP THINGS SIMPLE I WILL GO WITH THE MANDARIN SPELLING BEING THAT MANDARIN IS CHINA'S NATIONAL LANGUAGE. THE COMMON SENSE PRINCIPLES OF BUDDHISM SUCH AS THE NOBLE EIGHTFOLD PATH, THE FOUR NOBLE TRUTHS, AND CONCEPT OF KARMA HAVE PROVIDED ME WITH A POSITIVE OUTLET FOR DECISION MAKING. THE DAOIST BELIEF IN YIN AND YANG (POSITIVE/NEGATIVE), THE FOCUS ON THE ELEMENTS (EARTH, WIND, WATER, FIRE, METAL, WOOD), AND FENG SHUI (SPECIFIC PLACEMENT) HAS HELPED ME FIND HARMONY AND BALANCE. SHINTO IS A JAPANESE RELIGION SIMILAR TO DAOISM, IT'S FOCUS IS ON NATURE AND ONE'S ANCESTORS. ANCESTRY HAS ALWAYS BEEN IMPORTANT TO ME, SO I APPRECIATE THIS WAY OF THINKING. CONFUCIANISM IS BASED ON PHILOSOPHY AND THE CONCEPT OF A HIGHER EDUCATION, THIS GOES HAND IN HAND WITH MY LIFE'S PHILOSOPHY 'KAIZEN' THE JAPANESE WORD THAT MEANS BETTERMENT OR TO CONTINUOUSLY IMPROVE. THESE ASIAN BELIEF SYSTEMS ARE INTERCONNECTED, THEY ALL INFLUENCE EACH OTHER. AS A CHILD STUDYING MARTIAL ARTS I WAS FASCINATED BY PICTURES OF THE WARRIOR TEMPLE GUARDIANS AGYO AND UNGYO, THEY ARE PROMINENTLY SEEN AT SHINTO AND BUDDHIST TEMPLES THROUGHOUT JAPAN AND KOREA. AGYO'S MOUTH IS OPEN SYMBOLIZING YANG WHILE UNGYO'S MOUTH IS CLOSED SYMBOLIZING YIN, WHICH ILLUSTRATES THE DAOIST INFLUENCE. I ALSO APPRECIATED THE CULTURAL SIGNIFICANCE OF HACHIMAN, THE SHINTO GOD OF WAR, MOST IMAGES OF HIM SHOW HIM SEATED IN A BUDDHIST LIKE POSTURE, BECAUSE OF THIS HE IS OFTEN REFERRED TO AS 'BUDDHA-TO-BE'. THE THREE CHINESE DEITY'S THAT I INDENTIFY THE MOST WITH ARE GUAN YIN 'THE GODDESS OF COMPASSION', SUN WUKONG 'THE MONKEY KING', AND GUAN GONG THE FAMOUS CHINESE GENERAL. ALL THREE OF THESE DEITY'S ARE RECOGNIZED IN BOTH BUDDHISM AND DAOISM. GUAN YIN ,'THE GODDESS OF COMPASSION' IS ABOUT FORGIVENESS AND MERCY, IT IS SAID SHE CAN FEEL OTHERS PAIN AND SUFFERING. SUN WUKONG OR 'THE MONKEY KING' AS MOST PEOPLE KNOW HIM IS A MYTHICAL FIGURE OF LEGEND, HE HAS A REBELLIOUS SPIRIT AND IS A MASTER OF MARTIAL ARTS WITH UNPARALLELED SKILL, HE ALSO POSSESSES AN UNBREAKABLE WILL, LOOSING ONLY ONE BATTLE DUE TO TRICKERY. I PAY RESPECTS TO THE FAMOUS CHINESE GENERAL GUAN GONG BECAUSE HE WAS LOYAL TO HIS BROTHERS AND WILLING TO DIE IN ORDER TO FULFILL HIS OBLIGATIONS. WHEN GUAN GONG WAS ALIVE HE WAS RIGHTEOUS BEYOND ANY NORMAL MEASURE AND AN INDIVIDUAL OF THE HIGHEST INTEGRITY. THESE ARE CHARACTERISTICS I HOLD IN THE HIGHEST REGARD.

LAST BUT NOT LEAST I WOULD LIKE TO THANK MY PARENTS FOR LOVING AND SUPPORTING ME UNCONDITIONALLY THROUGH ALL THESE TRIALS AND TRIBULATIONS. TO MY IMMEDIATE FAMILY FOR ALWAYS BEING IN MY CORNER. I WOULD ALSO LIKE TO THANK MY BIG BROTHER IN ASIA, THE MAN I LOVE AND RESPECT ABOVE ALL OTHERS ; MY BROTHERS AND SISTERS FAR AND WIDE ; MY LONG TIME FRIENDS ; THE VIETNAMESE COMMUNITY THAT CONTINUES TO SHOW ME LOVE AND RESPECT TO THIS DAY ; AND TO EVERYONE ELSE THAT HAS SHOWN ME SUPPORT OVER THE YEARS. YOU ALL MADE THIS PROJECT A LOT MORE SATISFYING AND FOR THAT, I THANK YOU.

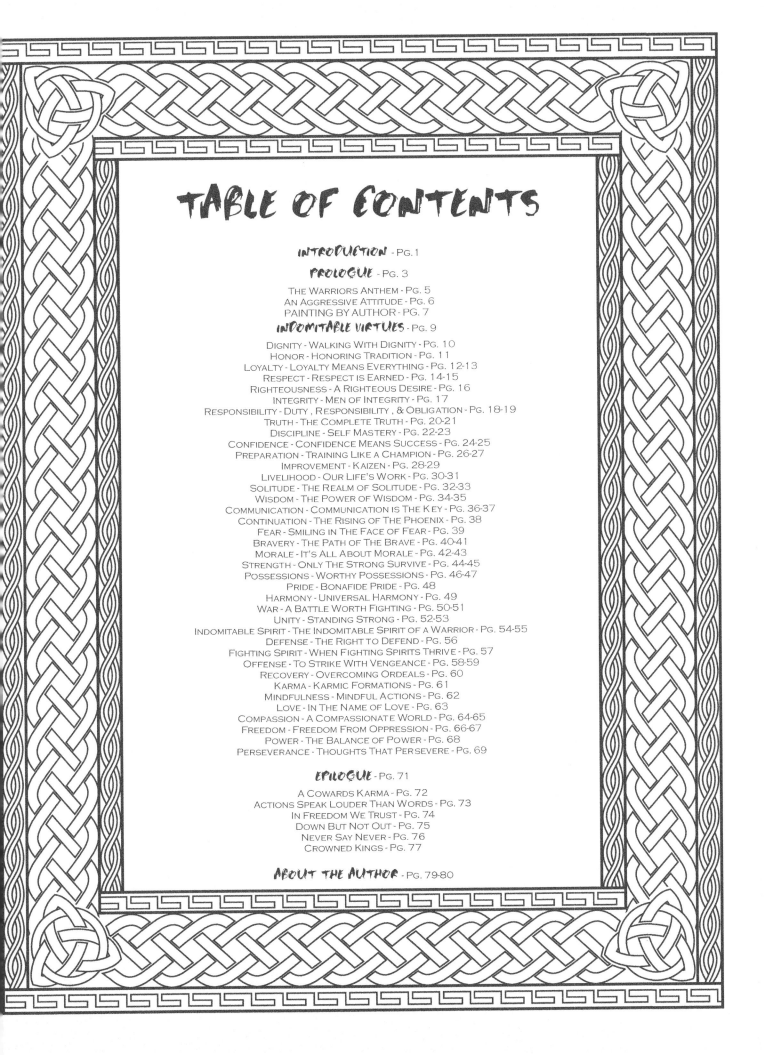

TABLE OF CONTENTS

INTRODUCTION

THIS BOOK WAS DESIGNED TO TAKE EACH VIRTUE MENTIONED AND SHOW THEM IN A POSITIVE LIGHT. SOME EXPRESSIONS MAY APPEAR MORE PERSONALIZED THAN OTHERS. PLEASE READ EACH VIRTUE LIKE YOU HAVE NOT READ THE OTHERS BEFORE THEM. WITH MANY VIRTUES BEING INTERRELATED SOME OF THE METHODS USED TO EMPHASIZE THEM MAY SEEM REPETITIVE. THIS IS NOT A "MUST ALL BE ALL" APPROACH BUT RATHER ONE MAN'S VIEW OF THE TOPICS DESCRIBED.

THERE IS NO LIMIT TO THE DIFFERENT APPLICATIONS OF THESE PRINCIPLES AND JUST LIKE EVERYTHING IN LIFE THEY CAN ALWAYS BE REFINED AND IMPROVED. THESE WORDS OF INSPIRATION MAY PROVIDE A SOLID FOUNDATION FOR THE READER TO WORK FROM. EACH VIRTUE IS DESCRIBED IN A THEMED SETTING SHOWING A WIDE RANGE OF CULTURAL APPLICATIONS AND THE AUTHOR'S MIND SET.

WITH EACH CIRCUMSTANCE THE COURSE OF ACTION CAN CHANGE. ALL THE WHILE THE AUTHOR IS TRYING TO INSPIRE A DESIRE, DEDICATION, AND DETERMINATION WITHIN THE READER SO THAT HIS INTERPRETATIONS CAN PROVIDE A POSITIVE OUTLOOK TOWARDS ANY OBSTACLES LIFE PASSES BY.

CREATING THIS TYPE OF ATTITUDE WILL ALLOW THE READER TO EXPERIENCE FIRST HAND THAT THOSE WORDS ARE WITHIN EACH VIRTUE. THE END RESULT IS UP TO THE READERS. THE AUTHOR'S ULTIMATE GOAL IS FOR THE READERS TO GAIN A CLEAR UNDERSTANDING OF THE POWER OF A POSITIVE MIND.

WITHIN EACH SETTING THERE IS SOME SYMBOLIC ARTISTRY, WHICH IS SIMPLY A FORM OF EXPRESSION WITHIN THE THEME. THIS PROVIDES A WIDER RANGE OF INTERPRETATIONS RATHER THAN A ONE DIMENSIONAL APPROACH. ALL THE DRAWINGS ARE EITHER DESIGNED BY OR ACTUALLY DRAWN BY THE AUTHOR HIMSELF. IF ONE SINGLE READER GAINS A BETTER PERSPECTIVE OF THE WORLD THEN THIS BOOK HAS BEEN A SUCCESS. FOR SOME THIS MAY BE A MODERN DAY SOLDIERS BIBLE. IT IS WITH OUR HUMBLE HOPES THAT THE READERS ENJOY THESE WORKS.

PROLOGUE

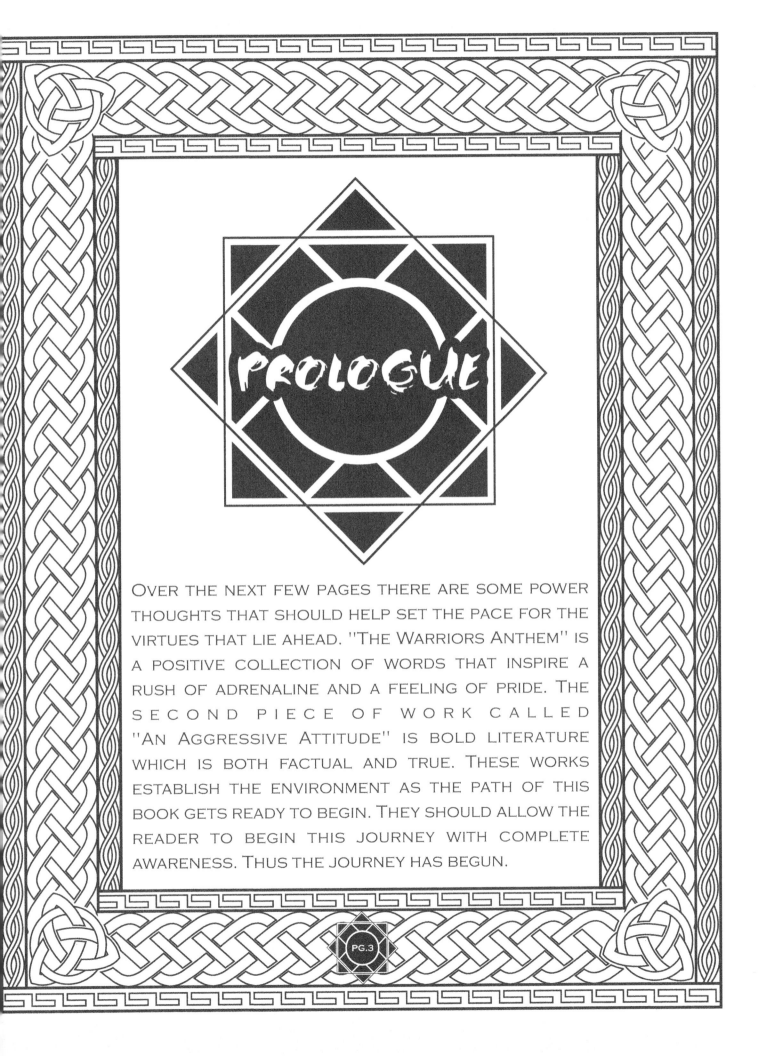

Over the next few pages there are some power thoughts that should help set the pace for the virtues that lie ahead. "The Warriors Anthem" is a positive collection of words that inspire a rush of adrenaline and a feeling of pride. The second piece of work called "An Aggressive Attitude" is bold literature which is both factual and true. These works establish the environment as the path of this book gets ready to begin. They should allow the reader to begin this journey with complete awareness. Thus the journey has begun.

THE WARRIORS ANTHEM

We desire to serve a divine purpose. A righteous one that makes us all feel honored. Our dedication to a cause defines who we are. Its all about Integrity & respect. With solidarity to begin and unity till the end, our choices are made with pride, there is no regret. As brothers we walk a journey full of triumph & tribulation. We are realistic, yet proud and optimistic. Willing to sacrifice to reach new heights. Victory has its rewards & the glory is our right. At the end of the day the feeling is great because we are brothers united for honor's sake.

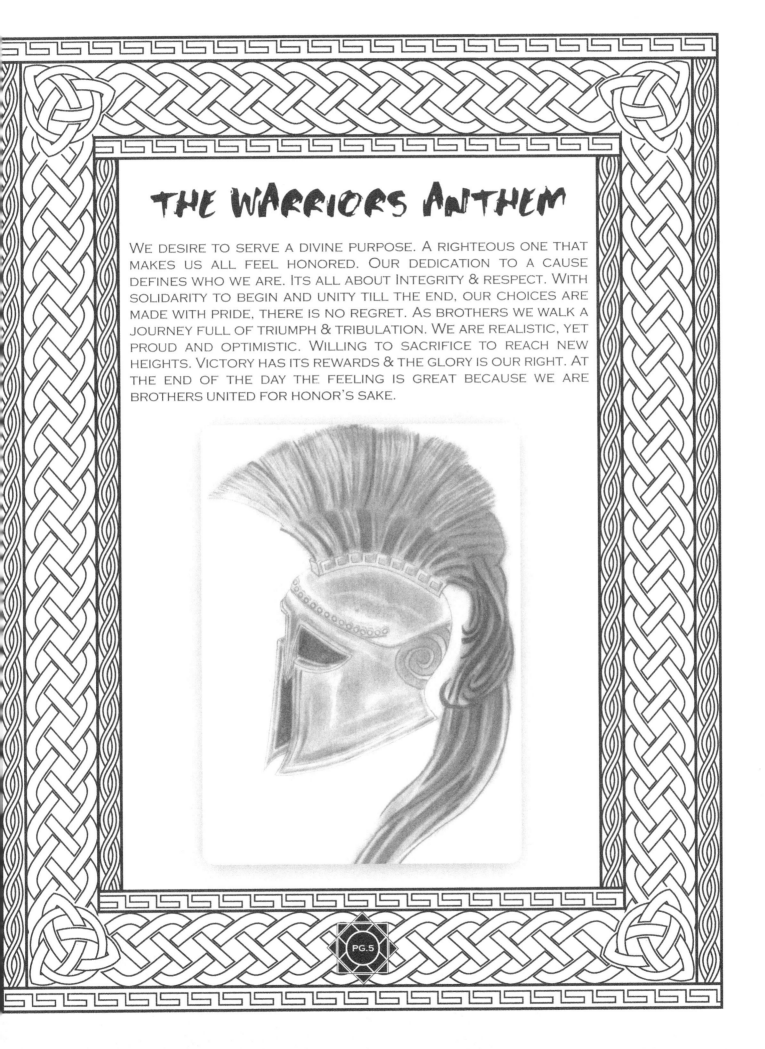

AN AGGRESSIVE ATTITUDE

OBTAIN ALL THE ESSENTIAL KNOWLEDGE THAT IS NEEDED TO BE A MASTER OF YOUR OWN ENVIRONMENT. DON'T ASSUME OR UNDERESTIMATE ANYTHING. BE LIKE THE WIND IT IS VERY DIFFICULT TO PLAN AGAINST FORMLESSNESS. ADAPT TO ALL CIRCUMSTANCES. HAVING THE BEST DEFENSE IS INVALUABLE, OFFENSE IS EASY. LEARN FROM THE MISTAKES OF OTHERS, FIX THE PROBLEM NOT THE BLAME. NO MATTER HOW BAD THINGS GET DON'T BE DISHEARTENED, BE MOTIVATED & NEVER LET UP. FOCUS ON AN AREA OF STRENGTH AND MAKE IT STRONGER. EXPECT THE UNEXPECTED ANYTHING CAN HAPPEN. IT IS BETTER TO HAVE WHAT YOU DON'T NEED THAN NEED WHAT YOU DON'T HAVE. THERE IS NO SUCH THING AS BEING PARANOID ITS CALLED BEING CAUTIOUS. THINK LONG TERM AND FOCUS ON WHAT IS WORKING. SAVE, INVEST WISELY, & DON'T PUT ALL YOUR EGGS IN ONE BASKET. STRIVE TO CONTINUOUSLY IMPROVE & BE THE BEST YOU CAN BE. PLAN PAST VICTORY, ONCE YOU HAVE ACHIEVED SUCCESS THE MOST IMPORTANT THING IS MAINTAINING IT. REMEMBER SUCCESS HAS A THOUSAND FATHERS BUT FAILURE IS AN ORPHAN!

Painting by Author

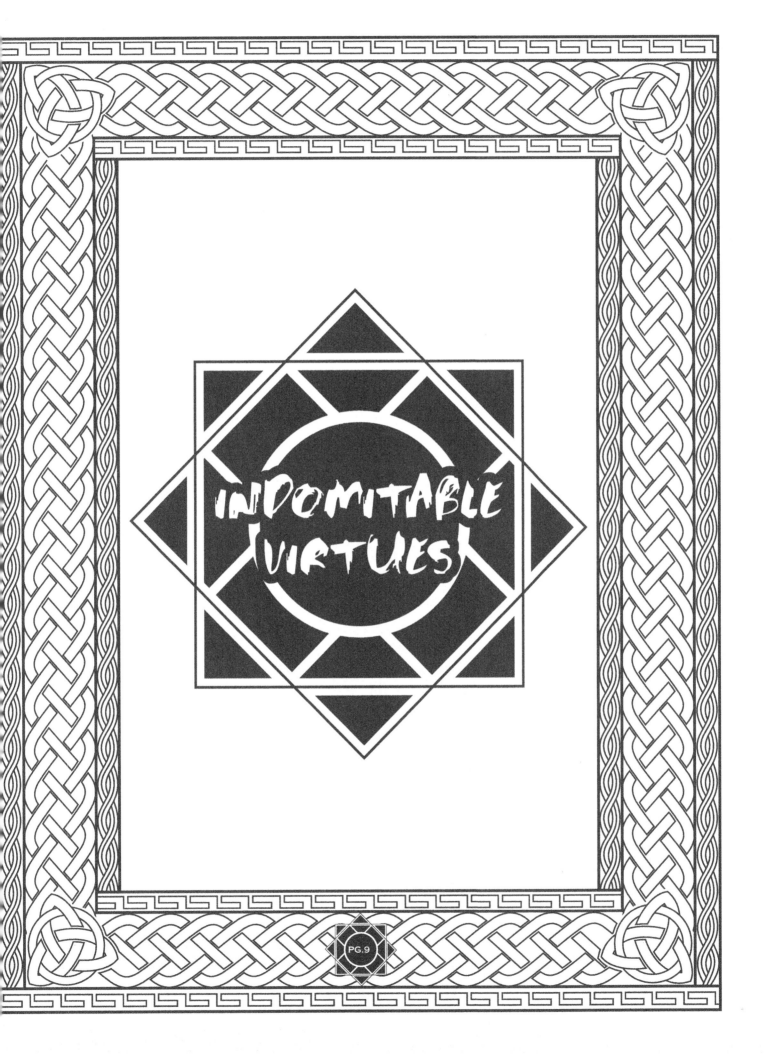

INDOMITABLE VIRTUES

WALKING WITH DIGNITY

WHAT WE THINK, SAY AND DO DEFINES WHO WE ARE. BEING FAIR, THOUGHTFUL AND RIGHTEOUS IS TO SHOW GOOD CHARACTER. BEING HUMBLE, HONEST AND TRUE, GUIDES US IN THE RIGHT DIRECTION. WE MUST DO OUR BEST TO FOLLOW THESE PRINCIPLES. THESE STANDARDS ARE WHAT SEPARATES US FROM EVERYONE ELSE. A NOBLE MAN WILL WALK WITH PRIDE AND DIGNITY UNDER ANY CIRCUMSTANCES. NO MATTER WHAT SITUATION WE ENCOUNTER THESE RULES IMPROVE THE LIFE WE LIVE.

HONORING TRADITION

As real men we are born with an instinct to uphold all the core principles set forth prior to our existence. Thus we inherit great responsibility. Out of respect we do our best to honor these traditions. Having a good name is celebrated. Therefore our word must be absolute. Additionally we cherish the opportunity to be in the presence of, and learn from the elite. It is an honored privilege to have these great masters teach us the skills necessary to be honorable men. Warriors are inspired and influenced by successful victors from the past. Setting higher standards makes achievements much more gratifying. Just like the Samurai's "Code of the Bushido" principles and beliefs become a guiding light. The feeling is fulfilling. Discipline is required to live by these principles. Once we choose this way of life it is our sworn obligation to be men of integrity, to show courage, and live up to our commitments. Honoring tradition is a path we all know, it has been set in stone.

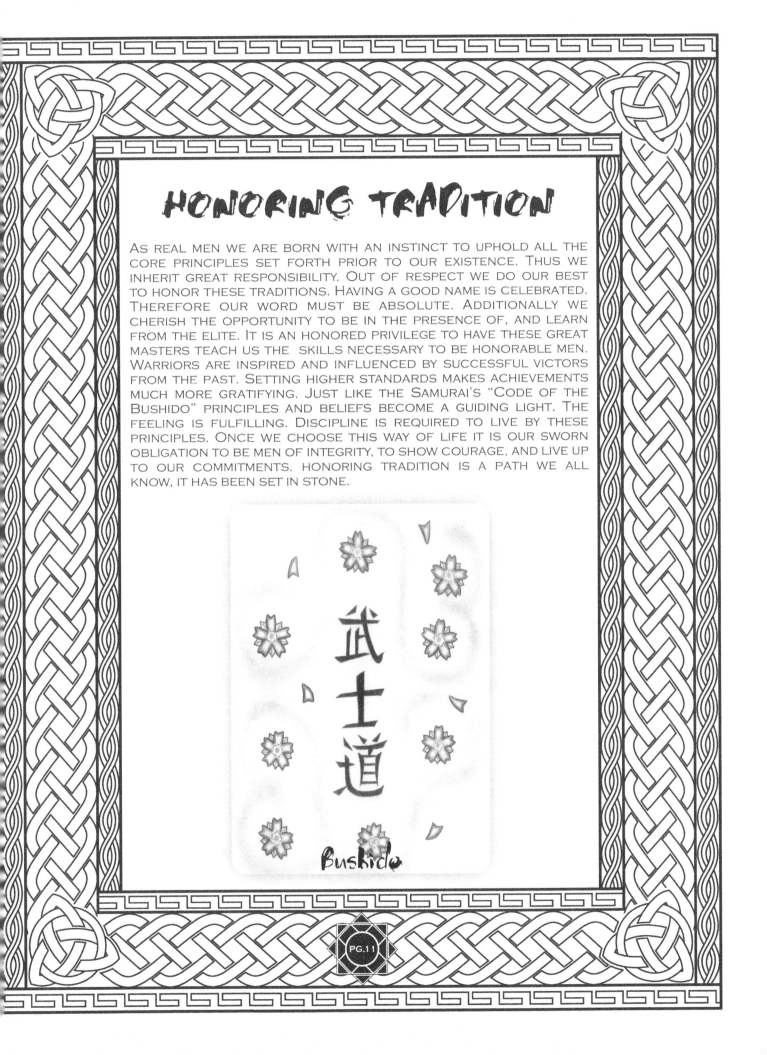

Bushido

忠誠

Guan Gong

LOYALTY MEANS EVERYTHING

Loyalty is invaluable. Being able to count on someone when times are tough, knowing you can trust someone, and having people support you no matter what your situation is a wonderful feeling. We feel pride and appreciation knowing, we are connected to people that possess these qualities. When someone's actions pledge their loyalty to us we feel happy and content. If we pledge our allegiance to a cause for a person we deem worthy, we gain a righteous satisfaction.

In life our loyalty is often tested. Attachments, distractions, and corruption can cause a man to fail. No one is beyond making errors. Men of power can be corrupted because of lust. They may love only one and their heart is loyal yet they become blinded by opportunities that present themselves. After these mistakes they feel guilt and regret.

In relationships forgiveness and dealing with everything as one union insures a much longer balanced relationship. We must accept accountability for our bad choices. An effort must be made so that bad influences cannot corrupt us. Let all negative thoughts and attachments blow away in the wind so they cannot poison the future.

One strength of loyalty is overcoming each other's shortcomings and misadventures. Through self cultivation and partnership a new level of growth develops. We reach a humble understanding. Thus inferior bonds become superior and strong bonds become stronger.

Whether it be for one's faith, the military, or a corporation; devotion, desire, and cooperation make all of our commitments much more fulfilling. A loyalty inspired confidence makes us act with temerity and helps us thrive with vigor. This creates a natural flow of continued positive productivity.

We must do everything in our power to remain loyal. Men must realize that without loyalty nothing lasts. It is the single most important factor for happiness, success and power. Loyalty means everything

Genghis Khan

RESPECT IS EARNED

Nothing in life is free. Constant dedication is required if we want to be dominant in our field of choice. Some learn the best methods. But others possess superior skills. Quality and consistency are important factors in accomplishing these goals. Having this type of knowledge helps us reach higher levels of achievement. The end result is the fruits of our labor. People respect productivity.

Our conduct reflects our character. We must give respect to earn respect. Respecting our elders, honoring our teachers and being a genuine person shows the type of man we are. Compassionate people stand out in a crowd. The wealthy that help the less fortunate are held in high regard. We feel an awesome aura in the presence of powerful people. These type of people leave a lasting impression. We value their influence.

Some people are excellent at expressing themselves. They encourage and motivate us with their words of wisdom. They make our achievements feel gratifying. They set standards in which we choose to follow. They show class even in defeat. These type of individuals continue to make their mark in history.

Disciplined people are an honor to witness. We are amazed by their strength, toughness and sheer determination. They achieve their goals, stay true to their word and devote themselves to meaningful causes. We are inspired by their code of ethics. We desire to be like them.

People respect what they have witnessed more than what they hear. No one's words of grandeur automatically earn our respect. We idolize dignified people. Learning from the best gives us an opportunity to follow the same path of achievement. With all being said we must strive to reach our full potential. Earning respect is entirely up to us, respect must be earned.

A Righteous Desire

A RIGHTEOUS MAN WILL FEEL GREAT INDIGNATION WHEN HE BEARS WITNESS TO THE DISHONORABLE INTENTIONS OF OTHERS. HE STANDS UP FOR EVERYTHING THAT IS JUST. GIVING TO THOSE IN NEED, PROTECTING THE DEFENSELESS, AND FIGHTING FOR WHAT'S RIGHT DESCRIBE HIS CHARACTER. HONOR, LOYALTY, AND RESPECT ARE PART OF WHO HE IS. ALL HIS ACTIONS ARE DONE WITH DIGNITY. HE IS THE EPITOME OF INTEGRITY.

HE WILL LISTEN WHOLEHEARTEDLY WITHOUT BIAS AND TRY TO RESOLVE ALL PROBLEMS TO THE BEST OF HIS ABILITY. HE WILL RISK HIS LIFE TO KEEP HIS PROMISES. HIS WORD IS HIS BOND TO THIS WORLD. HE WILL GIVE WHAT IS HIS TO PEOPLE THAT NEED IT MORE BECAUSE IT BRINGS HIM JOY. HE IS VERY GRATEFUL TO HAVE ANY OPPORTUNITY TO HELP. WHEN SOMEONE IS TAKEN ADVANTAGE OF HE WILL STAND UP AND SPEAK OUT WITH PASSION. WHEN BOUNDARIES ARE CROSSED AND VICTIMS PAINED HE SEEKS RETRIBUTION WITH AN UNRELENTING DETERMINATION.

THE ODDS DON'T MATTER TO HIM. NO MATTER WHAT HE IS THERE TO HELP, ESPECIALLY WHEN NO ONE ELSE IS. HE WILL LEAD A RESURGENCE OVER AND OVER AGAIN. KNOWING HE IS RIGHT FUELS HIS INNER BEING. NOTHING CAN STOP HIS DESIRE TO DO WHAT MUST BE DONE. IN DEATH HIS CONTRIBUTIONS ARE IMMORTALIZED.

MEN OF INTEGRITY

THE MOST IDOLIZED AND RESPECTED MEN IN THE WORLD OFTEN HAVE SELFLESS ATTITUDES AND GENUINE INTENTIONS. THESE MEN REFLECT A SENSE OF PURITY AND TRUTH.

THEY HAVE A WAY WITH WORDS THAT HELPS US UNDERSTAND "THEIR" MEANING WITH CLARITY. THEIR ACTIONS ARE A PERFECT EXPRESSION OF THEIR CHARACTER. THROUGH THEIR HEARTFELT PASSION WE GET A GRASP OF WHAT THEY TRULY THINK AND FEEL.

WHEN SOMEONE'S WELL-BEING IS THEIR RESPONSIBILITY THEY ARE REASONABLE, HONEST AND FAIR. THEY WILL NOT ALLOW ANY NEGATIVE INFLUENCES TO MAKE THEM BIASED. THEY ARE THEIR OWN MAN AND MAKE THEIR OWN DECISIONS. THEY ENVISION THE SITUATION FROM ALL ANGLES AND NEVER RUSH THEIR JUDGMENT. MANY PEOPLE FALSELY CLAIM TO BE THESE TYPE OF MEN. IMITATIONS ALWAYS GET EXPOSED. REAL MEN NEVER CHANGE THEIR VALUES AND ALWAYS REMAIN THE SAME. THEY ARE A RARE BREED WHOSE INTEGRITY WILL ALWAYS SHINE THROUGH.

THESE MEN ARE RIGHTEOUS AND DIGNIFIED. THEY ARE COURTEOUS ALWAYS MAKING AN EFFORT TO MAKE PEOPLE FEEL RESPECTED AND APPRECIATED. THEY HAVE THE HIGHEST VALUES WHICH IS USUALLY A STRONG REFLECTION OF THEIR BELIEFS. THEY DO EVERYTHING FROM THE HEART AND HAVE ABSOLUTE LOYALTY TO WHATEVER CAUSE THEY HOLD DEAR. THESE MEN OF INTEGRITY HONOR THEIR WORD AND PROSPER BECAUSE THEY UNSELFISHLY DO WHAT'S BEST FOR THE GOOD OF ALL.

RESPONSIBILITY, DUTY and OBLIGATION

When a battle is worth fighting, men with supremacy of character step forward. They have an unrestrained passion for a noble cause, it is their sole purpose in life. Their integrity is unquestionable. They are dignified, achieving power is not their plan. They value principles above all else. They will provide for and protect everything and everyone they hold dear. They are duty bound to honor their commitments. Their word is iron. They are the type of men that feel an obligation to serve the cause wholeheartedly. They hold themselves responsible and accept accountability if they fail. They are masters of skill and have a powerful desire to exceed all expectations. They capitalize on the opportunity to serve. Their devotion ensures efficiency and unity within the ranks. They are brave valorous men. They put the well being of others before their own. Their self sacrifice is known. With each breath they cherish their duty. Their blood flows so they can live by the code.

THE COMPLETE TRUTH

EXPERIENCE, COMMON SENSE AND KNOWLEDGE ARE THREE WAYS TO SEEK THE TRUTH. THROUGH LIFE'S EXPERIENCES WE LEARN ABOUT DISAPPOINTMENT, DENIAL AND FEAR. WE ALSO EXPERIENCE HAPPINESS, REALIZATION AND CONFIDENCE. COMMON SENSE IS UNDERSTOOD THROUGH CONCEPTS, REASONING AND ANALYSIS. KNOWLEDGE COMES FROM HISTORY AND FACTUAL UNDERSTANDING. THERE IS ALSO A KNOWLEDGE WITHIN. DREAMS AND VISIONS CAN GIVE ONE PERCEPTIONS OF ABSOLUTE CERTAINTY.

AWARENESS, ACCEPTANCE AND APPRECIATION HELP US GRASP THE TRUTH. WHEN IT COMES TO MATTERS OF THE HEART WE CAN EXPERIENCE TRUE LOVE OR UNCOVER BROKEN PROMISES AND BETRAYAL. THUS THESE CIRCUMSTANCES HELP US GAIN WISDOM FROM THE TRUTH.

FROM CHILDHOOD WE ARE TAUGHT WHAT IS RIGHT AND WRONG, WHICH BECOMES A NATURAL WAY TO REACT TO WHATEVER SITUATION WE ENCOUNTER. WE LEARN ABOUT HONESTY, MAKING THE RIGHT CHOICES, AND WHAT IS PROPER CONDUCT. THIS ALLOWS US TO SEE THE REAL STATE OF THINGS WITH CLARITY.

WE FEEL A CALMING GRATITUDE WHEN WE KNOW WHAT WE BELIEVE IS TRUE. OUR PURITY OF FAITH MAKES US BRAVE AND GIVES US COURAGE. WE MUST LEARN THE TRUTH SO WE HAVE PROPER GUIDANCE FOR WHATEVER TASK WE CHOOSE. WHAT WE FEEL, HOW WE COMMUNICATE AND OUR ACTIONS ARE MUCH MORE MEANINGFUL WHEN THEY ARE GENUINE AND TRUE. THE TRUTH IS PURE. IT REMOVES ALL CONTAMINATION AND CORRUPTION. BY KNOWING THE TRUTH WE GAIN A POWERFUL POSITIVE OUTLOOK ON LIFE, THIS MAKES US FEEL COMPLETE

SELF MASTERY

A Disciplined Warrior Will Always :

Train like a Spartan and never under estimate anyone.

Give respect and never disrespect.

Be humble and never be conceded.

Gather information and
never react without knowing the facts.

Have a backup plan and never assume anything.

Strive to learn new things and never be close minded.

Be ready and never let his guard down.

Stand strong and never show fear.

Push forward and never give up.

Appreciate victory and never gloat.

Be a worthy champion, respecting his title
and never forgetting the fact that somebody
will always want to take it.

CONFIDENCE MEANS SUCCESS

BEING ABLE TO TUNE OUT ALL NEGATIVE COMMENTS AND THE DOUBT THEY CREATE IS NOT EASY. HOWEVER AS WE CONSISTENTLY PERFORM THE SAME TASK SUCCESSFULLY WE FEEL A SENSE OF SURENESS. OUR KNOWLEDGE AND EXPERIENCE DETERMINES HOW WE REACT. REACHING HIGHER LEVELS OF ACHIEVEMENT GIVES US THE EDGE WE NEED TO SUCCEED. WHEN WE ARE FAMILIAR WITH WHAT'S IN FRONT OF US WE ACT ACCORDINGLY. OUR PERFORMANCE PRACTICALLY BECOMES INFALLIBLE. THUS CONFIDENCE IS BORN.

WE MUST ELIMINATE SELF-DOUBT. BY CONFRONTING THE ELEMENTS THAT CAUSE DISCOMFORT WE CAN LEARN TO EMBRACE THEM RATHER THAN FEAR THEM. OVERCOMING THESE OBSTACLES MAKES US STRONGER. AS MEN WE HAVE THE ABILITY TO TAKE AN AREA OF WEAKNESS AND MAKE IT A STRENGTH.

IN MANY CASES PEOPLE ARE BORN WITH GIFTS THAT GIVE THEM AN EDGE. SOME PEOPLE ARE VERY INTELLIGENT OR CREATIVE. OTHERS MAY BE FAST, STRONG OR ABLE TO ENDURE FOR LONG PERIODS OF TIME. BY RECOGNIZING THESE ASSETS A MAN CAN EMBRACE AND HONE HIS SKILLS. BY LEARNING FROM EXPERTS IN A FIELD AND WITH HANDS ON TRAINING WE GAIN INVALUABLE EXPERIENCE. OUR SKILLS IMPROVING AND BEING RECOGNIZED INSPIRES US. THIS GIVES A LEARNED MAN CONFIDENCE IN AREAS THAT PERTAIN TO HIS CHOSEN FIELD.

IN A GAME OF POKER THE LOOK ON A MAN'S FACE CAN HELP HIS GAME. IT CAN ENCOURAGE HIS OPPONENT TO MAKE THE WRONG JUDGMENT. JUST LIKE A WARRIOR HAVING A STONE FACE EXPRESSION DURING COMBAT GIVES HIS OPPONENT A FEELING OF DOUBT AND FEAR. HAVING THE LOOK OF CONFIDENCE IS A POWER ALL IN ITSELF. SILENCE IS ALSO A POWERFUL TOOL THAT CAN BE USED TO GAIN RESPECT AND INSPIRE CONFIDENCE. SILENCE ALLOWS US A LONGER TIME TO THINK ABOUT WHAT IS THE BEST COURSE OF ACTION, WHICH CONTRIBUTES TO MAKING STRONG DECISIONS.

THROUGH REPETITIVE PRACTICE WE BECOME ONE WITH ALL ASPECTS OF WHATEVER TYPE OF SKILLS WE ARE TRYING TO ACQUIRE. OUR PERFORMANCE BECOMES AS NATURAL AS THE FLOW OF WATER. BY PERFECTING ALL THE METHODS REQUIRED IN OUR FIELD OF CHOICE WE GAIN THE CONFIDENCE THAT IS NEEDED TO PREVAIL. THIS ENSURES THAT WE WILL NEVER SECOND-GUESS WHAT NEEDS TO BE DONE. WITHOUT CONFIDENCE SUCCESS IS RARE.

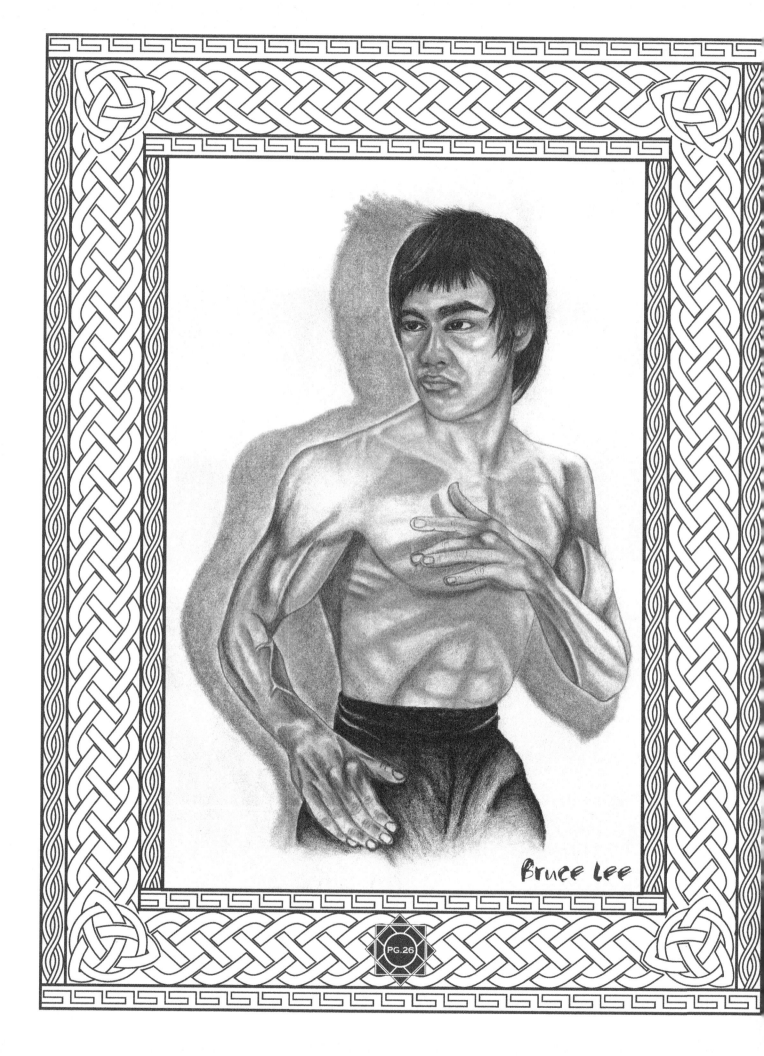

Bruce Lee

TRAINING LIKE A CHAMPION

Throughout history great nations and legendary individuals have set almost inhumane standards of achievement. They went beyond normal measures to ensure the best results. Their skills and preparedness was second to none.

The Mongols had elite skills on horseback. The samurai used their swords as an extension of there being. The Spartan's will power and sheer determination on the battlefield can still be felt to this day. The legendary Bruce Lee's fanatical relentless pursuit of the ultimate realization of combat set the foundation for modern-day martial arts. These individuals were disciplined, dedicated and performed with unimaginable intensity. They worked smarter and harder giving their all, all the time. This is what made the difference.

Our mind set is an important tool that provides a path towards victory. Being mentally acute makes our reactions crisp and effective. Having a never quit attitude helps us keep pushing forward. A calm mind allows us to think rationally and clear. Being emotionally content inspires confidence. Thus we can use a winning strategy and apply the best tactics.

Physical training involves strength, endurance and skill. Training should focus on quality and efficiency. Being strong and having your body conditioned to withstand the tasks we need to perform is a necessity. In combat we must have already applied what we know to truly understand every element completely. The reality must be experienced so we learn timing and the right solutions to any obstacles we face.

Being a step ahead is the edge we need to be ready for when the moment really matters. We must give the extra that is needed and train like a champion so we can reach our full potential. Mastering the skills of our chosen field gives us the confidence we need to succeed.

改善

KAIZEN

Like a Koi fish proudly jumping out of the water on a beautiful day we appreciate it's passion to rise to the highest level.

Kaizen is a Japanese term that means to continuously improve. This mindset translates to a powerful winning philosophy.

Everything in the universe evolves. There is an energy constantly moving forward. Within every environment there is always a way to refine and improve the atmosphere. Unlocking this key is a sacred treasure. There are unlimited avenues this can be applied to. Through discovery, dedication, and consistency a higher level can be achieved. Absorbing all this available knowledge creates diversity. With art, one gets more creative, clothing designs reach new levels of appeal, automobiles get marketed and sold more efficiently, all because of the positive attitude that is created. Thoughts, ideas, and beliefs reach new heights. It's about eliminating waste and working smarter not harder. Taking the best elements of whatever field and forming a superior product or better way of doing things. The work place becomes a house of harmony. In group situations teamwork and morale become as natural as breathing. You are surrounded by successful people with the same goals. It is a constant triumph. Ideas for improvement and personal discipline become contagious. This is a taste of what can be obtained. Kaizen is a sacred treasure that must be cherished, it is a way of life with no limit to its depth.

OUR LIFE'S WORK

OUR DESTINY IS INFLUENCED BY OUR FAMILY LIFE, WHAT WE STRIVE FOR, AND HOW WE MAKE A LIVING. IT IS UP TO US TO TAKE THE INITIATIVE SO WE CAN MAKE THE MOST OF OUR CHOICES. OUR VITALITY DEPENDS ON IT.

THERE ARE DIFFERENT ASPECTS OF FAMILY LIFE. SOME PEOPLE ARE CONTENT HAVING SUPPORT FROM THEIR PARENTS AND SIBLINGS OR BY SIMPLY HAVING A PARTNER. OTHERS WISH TO START A FAMILY OF THEIR OWN. FOR SOME, HAVING CHILDREN HELPS COMPLETE THEIR CYCLE OF LIFE, MAKING IT MORE FULFILLING. IN EITHER SCENARIO THEY FEEL SATISFIED. IT MAKES ALL TYPES OF CELEBRATIONS WONDERFUL AND REWARDING. BEING HAPPY AND CONTENT CONTRIBUTES TO HARMONY IN ONE'S HOME.

WHAT WE STRIVE FOR BECOMES OUR PURPOSE IN LIFE. WE OFTEN HAVE OTHER INTERESTS OUTSIDE OUR DAILY DUTIES. IT COULD BE SUPPORTING A CAUSE, GOING ON A LIFE-CHANGING JOURNEY, OR SOME TYPE OF TRAINING. WHATEVER THE SITUATION, THESE EXPERIENCES CAN SATISFY OUR SELF INTEREST. THEY MAKE OUR OCCUPATION MORE REWARDING AND ESTABLISH A PATH TOWARDS WHAT TRULY INSPIRES US.

HOW WE MAKE A LIVING CAN BE VERY REWARDING AND IMPROVE ASPECTS OF OUR LIFE. ENJOYING WHAT WE DO IS AN EXCEPTIONAL GIFT. OBTAINING THE HIGHEST EXPECTATIONS CAN BE TRYING BUT IT SETS STANDARDS OF ACHIEVEMENT THAT MOTIVATE US TO WORK HARDER. THIS COMPETITIVE FACTOR BRINGS OUT THE BEST IN US.

COMPLETE SATISFACTION DOES NOT HAPPEN OVERNIGHT. THIS IS SOMETHING WE SPEND OUR ENTIRE LIFE TRYING TO ACQUIRE. LIKE THEY SAY "ROME WASN'T BUILT IN A DAY," IT WAS BUILT BRICK BY BRICK OVER TIME. IN THE END WE DESIRE TO BE ABLE TO LOOK BACK ON EVERY ASPECT OF OUR LIFE'S WORK AND KNOW WE DID EVERYTHING WE COULD AND GAVE IT OUR ALL.

SOLITUDE

THE REALM OF SOLITUDE

How we spend our time is entirely up to us. We need not be dependent on anyone. We live our own life. We start each day standing alone. The need for someone to talk with is simply a craving, not a necessity. We enjoy the company of others but we do not need to depend on it for happiness.

We can create our own environment. Having this wisdom enables us to embrace alone time rather than fear it. Our ego wants someone to talk with. Don't crave what you can't have.

Loneliness is a negative concept. There is an awesome power created from silence. Exercise these skills and your character will become stronger.

Solitude is a realm that encourages deep thinking. This allows us to consolidate everything that has worth. Through self-discovery and heightened awareness we see everything with clarity thus we realize the value of time we spend alone.

Being self sufficient is a positive way to live a productive lifestyle. Life is too short to spend waiting on others. There is nothing wrong with walking and eating alone. We can keep ourselves entertained. We can perform our tasks with passion. We can welcome these experiences and learn to cherish them.

We control our feelings. We must have the right perception. See the beauty in the present. Allow our future to look bright. Accept who we are. Be who we are. Let this be our will. We can live our moments alone as if they are a Devine opportunity to improve the life we live.

THE POWER OF WISDOM

Knowledge, experiences, and patience are traits true to wisdom. Knowing what is required of us, having been through a crisis, or mental toughness helps us deal with life's circumstances.

Life means suffering. From the moment we are born we experience the pain of hunger. As we grow we learn to crave, want, and need. Attachments are the origin of suffering. We can stop this by powers of the mind. We must be willing to let go of all that causes us pain. Only then can we stop this suffering. Once we realize this, everything is viewed in a different light. Learning from the mistakes of others helps us live a more prosperous life. Happiness and contentment cannot be purchased. Our actions lead us toward the path we have chosen. We hold the key to our future.

Everything we do has some type of reaction. Life is a continuous cycle. The wise know war causes pain so they try to teach people to view the value of peace. Ignorance is sad. Holidays, seasons, and celebrations are wonderful times in which the older generation teach the young about the past customs and traditions. History always repeats itself.

As we are educated about life's wonders we must be humble. Conceit opens the door for failure. Distinguished people overcome many obstacles to achieve what they desire. We must be patient so that we can persevere.

History is valuable. Experiences of the past gives us knowledge for the future. Everything comes into perspective. This enables us to enjoy living life to the fullest. Our minds are the key to overcoming all these obstacles. Thus we can truly understand the power of wisdom

COMMUNICATION IS THE KEY

EXPRESSION, NEGOTIATION, AND COMPROMISE ARE METHODS WE USE TO COMMUNICATE. TO EFFECTIVELY EXCEL IN THESE AREAS WE MUST HAVE A CLEAR UNDERSTANDING OF HOW AN INDIVIDUAL VIEWS A SITUATION AND WHAT THEIR INTENTIONS ARE. COMMUNICATION IS AN ONGOING PROCESS. WHETHER IT'S FAMILY, BUSINESS OR EVERYDAY ENCOUNTERS WE CONTINUALLY EXPERIENCE THE NEED TO GET THE RIGHT MESSAGE ACROSS. PATIENCE, CONFIDENCE, AND CHARM ARE GREAT TOOLS FOR SELF-EXPRESSION. AN EFFECTIVE COMMUNICATOR CAN MAKE ANY SITUATION A BETTER ONE.

EMOTION CAN CREATE A HOSTILE ENVIRONMENT. WE MUST DO OUR BEST TO REMAIN CALM AND DISARM HOSTILITY TO AVOID A NEGATIVE OUTCOME. PATIENCE IS NEEDED TO PROPERLY ANALYZE EVERY DETAIL OF WHAT A PERSON IS TRYING TO STRESS. REACTING TOO QUICKLY LIMITS OUR POTENTIAL TO UNDERSTAND COMPLETELY. FIRE AGAINST FIRE CREATES A BIGGER FLAME. SILENCE IS LIKE ADDING WATER TO THE FLAMES. THIS LIMITED REACTION WILL CALM THINGS CONSIDERABLY.

WE CAN EDUCATE THE OPPOSITION THROUGH PEACEFUL EXPRESSION. BY CREATING A FACTUAL PICTURE EVERYTHING BECOMES MORE CLEAR. OUR FINESSE CAN HELP THEM ANSWER OUR QUESTIONS PRODUCTIVELY. THEIR INVOLVEMENT TAKES THE EDGE OFF. WHEN THEY AGREE WITH THEIR OWN ANSWERS THEY DON'T FEEL THREATENED. FURTHERMORE BOTH SIDES SHARING THE SAME VIEW GREATLY ELIMINATE BIAS.

IN NEGOTIATIONS BOTH SIDES HAVE THEIR OWN OBJECTIVES. EACH SIDE ENTERS DISCUSSIONS WITH A GOAL IN MIND. KNOWING EACH OTHER'S INTENTIONS IS THE TRICKY PART. IN BUSINESS THE OTHER SIDE WILL OFTEN USE TACTICS. SOME TRY TO STRONG-ARM AND SHOW NO FLEXIBILITY, SO ONE MUST BE LIKE WATER AND FIND A WAY PAST THEIR WALL. OTHERS ARE AGGRESSIVE AND SLANDEROUS. WE MUST DEFLECT AND DIFFUSE THEIR ATTACKS. LASTLY SOME TRY TO TRICK OR MISLEAD US. WE MUST SHINE A LIGHT ON WHAT THEY ARE TRYING TO DO. A FAIR PLAYING FIELD MAKES A NEGOTIATED AGREEMENT A STRONGER POSSIBILITY.

THERE ARE MANY WAYS FOR BOTH PARTIES TO COMPROMISE AND REACH A MUTUAL UNDERSTANDING. THE ANSWERS TO SOME QUESTIONS CAN PROVIDE A PATH TOWARDS AGREEMENT. WHAT ARE OF MUTUAL INTEREST? WHAT ARE THE AVAILABLE OPTIONS? WHAT TYPE OF STANDARDS HAVE BEEN SET? ARE THERE ALTERNATIVES? USING THESE GUIDELINES HELPS US COME UP WITH A MORE REALISTIC PROPOSAL. THIS ALLOWS US TO TAKE A CERTAIN PERSPECTIVE AND REINFORCES IT IN A DIFFERENT LIGHT. WHICH CAN MAKE EVERYTHING MORE APPEALING FOR EVERYONE INVOLVED. A POSITIVE ATMOSPHERE WORKS WONDERS.

MORE OFTEN THAN NOT SOMEONE BEING OVERLY AGGRESSIVE WILL CREATE AN EXTREMELY DEFENSIVE ENVIRONMENT. THIS LIMITS THE CHANCE FOR A REASONABLE OUTCOME. WHEN EVERYTHING MOVES TOO FAST IT CAN MAKE SOMEONE FEEL OVERWHELMED. THEY WILL STALL FOR SAFETY TO MAKE SURE THEY DID NOT MISS SOMETHING. FEAR OF LOSING FACE IS OFTEN THE MAIN REASON AGREEMENTS ARE NOT MADE. LET THE OTHER SIDE FEEL CONTENT. WHEN BOTH PARTIES ARE MUTUALLY SATISFIED EVERYONE WINS. COMMUNICATION IS THE KEY TO OVERCOMING THESE LIMITATIONS.

THE RISING OF A PHOENIX

SOMETIMES OUR LIVES HAVE BALANCE AND OTHER TIMES THEY ARE A CLASSICAL MESS. WE TRY TO UNITE THE POSITIVE AND NEGATIVE ELEMENTS TO FORM A BALANCE. AS TIME GOES BY WE EITHER FIX THE PROBLEM OR FIND A WAY TO GET PAST IT.

IN RELATIONSHIPS AND MARRIAGE WE STRIVE TO LIVE A HARMONISTIC LIFESTYLE. WE DESIRE TO MAKE HAPPINESS AND CONTENTMENT A CONTINUOUS CYCLE, SO THE FLAME NEVER STOPS BURNING.

DEALING WITH ALL TYPES OF SITUATIONS IS A STEP IN THE RIGHT DIRECTION. FROM THIS WE CAN REEVALUATE OUR OUTLOOK. THUS WE CAN VISUALIZE THE BEST POSSIBLE SOLUTIONS.

THROUGH THESE EXPERIENCES WE LEARN TO OVERCOME OUR VULNERABILITIES AND INSECURITIES. AS INDIVIDUALS WE GROW. NO MATTER WHAT HAPPENS WE ALWAYS FIND A WAY TO PICK OURSELVES BACK UP. THE NEGATIVE ASPECTS OF THE PAST BURN INTO FLAMES AND OFFER US A NEW BEGINNING.

LIBERATION, FULFILMENT, AND COMPLETION ARE THE FORCE THAT DRIVES US TO FINISH WHAT WE START. IT IS THE SOURCE THAT CAUSES PHYSICAL AND SPIRITUAL TRANSFORMATIONS. THIS IS THE POWER THAT RECONSTRUCTS NATIONS AND EMPIRES, REGENERATING PAST SYMBOLS OF PROSPERITY WITH AN INFINITE CONTINUATION LIKE THE RESURRECTION OF A PHOENIX FROM ITS ASHES.

不死鳥

SMILING IN THE FACE OF FEAR

FEAR IS VERY POWERFUL, IT CAN DESTROY A MAN OR HELP HIM DO THINGS HE NEVER THOUGHT WERE POSSIBLE. ANY REAL MAN WILL ADMIT HE HAS FELT FEAR BEFORE SOME TYPE OF CONFRONTATIONAL SITUATION WHETHER IT BE COMBAT OR A COMPETITION.

BEING SCARED IS OK AS LONG AS WE STILL HAVE THE COURAGE TO DO OUR DUTY. SOME MEN SMILE IN THE FACE OF FEAR, WHILE OTHERS WEAR A MASK THAT SHOWS NO EMOTION. PEOPLE FEAR MANY THINGS SUCH AS HELPLESSNESS, FAILURE, AND REJECTION. SOME FEAR RUTHLESS PEOPLE OR PUNISHMENT THAT COULD COME DUE TO THEIR ACTIONS. OTHERS FEAR GOD OR BAD KARMA.

ACKNOWLEDGEMENT, UNDERSTANDING, AND ACCEPTANCE WILL CLARIFY OUR FEARS. ONCE WE RECOGNIZE OUR FEARS A PORTAL TO REALITY WILL BE OPENED. IF WE GIVE IN TO FEAR WE CEASE TO TRULY LIVE. SOCIETY TEACHES US TO FEAR MANY THINGS, WE MUST THINK FOR OURSELVES AND CONTROL OUR OWN FATE. FEAR CAN CAUSE SELF DOUBT AND HESITATION, WHICH IS WHY WE MUST BE BOLD. FEAR CAN ALSO CAUSE COWARDICE AND DESPAIR, SO WE MUST BE BRAVE. LASTLY FEAR CAN CAUSE PAIN, SUFFERING AND DEFEAT THEREFORE WE MUST BE STRONG AND SHOW COURAGE SO THAT WE CAN SMILE IN THE FACE OF FEAR.

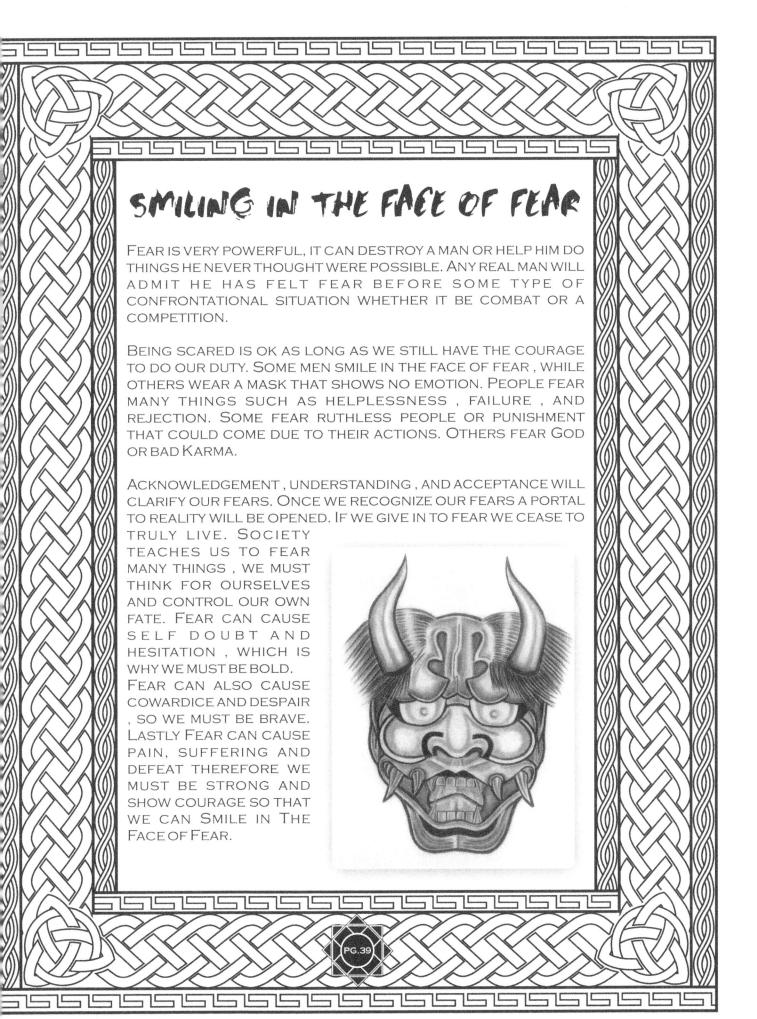

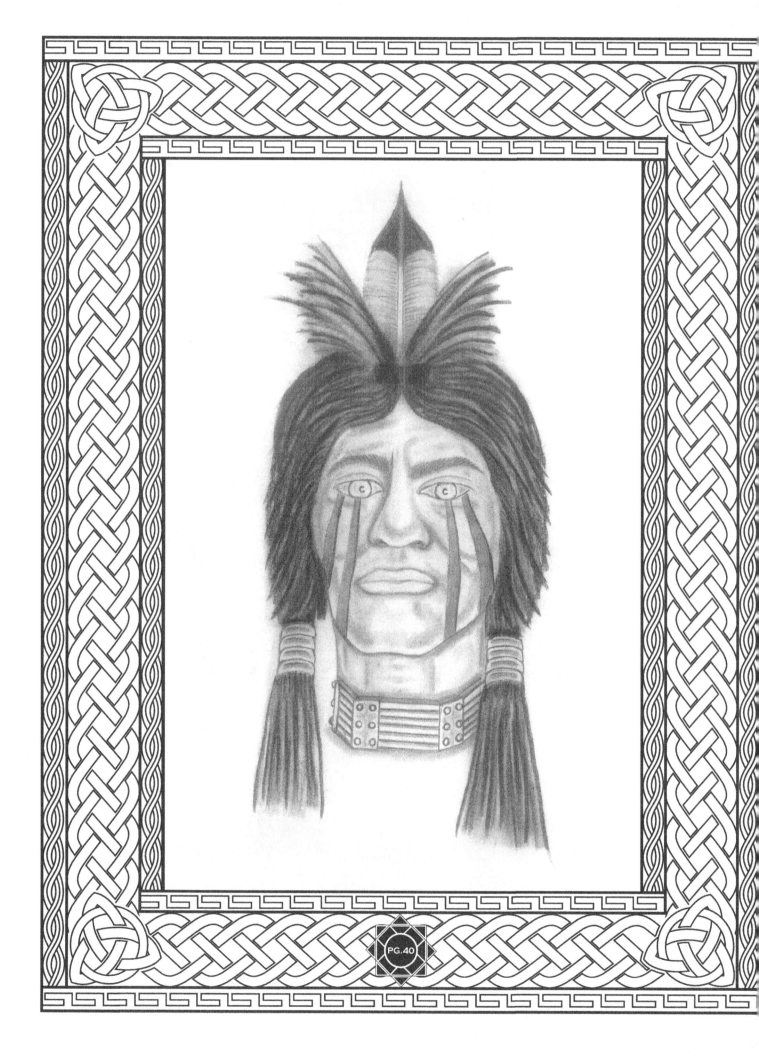

THE PATH OF THE BRAVE

BRAVE MEN TAKE EVERYTHING TO THE NEXT LEVEL. IF IT WASN'T FOR THE TEMERITY OF THESE MEN OUR ACHIEVEMENTS WOULD BE VERY LIMITED. SINCE THE BEGINNING OF MAN THESE WARRIORS HAVE LED THE WAY. HOWEVER BRAVE MEN ARE NOT LIMITED TO WARRIORS. THERE HAS BEEN LIVES SAVED AND MAJOR ADVANCES IN TECHNOLOGY BY MEN WILLING TO GO AGAINST THE ODDS FOR THE GOOD OF ALL.

SOMETIMES A MAN'S FATE HAS ALREADY BEEN DECIDED. FROM THE MOMENT HE IS BORN HE HAS RECOGNIZABLE TRAITS. AS HE GROWS THEY CONTINUALLY DEVELOP. HE WILL EMBRACE HIS DESTINY. CONSTANT PRACTICE AND TRAINING IS NECESSARY FOR HIM TO DEVELOP HIS SKILLS. THIS KNOWLEDGE WILL HELP HIM REACH LEVELS NEVER THOUGHT POSSIBLE. THIS CONSTANT PREPARATION GIVES HIM THE CONFIDENCE HE NEEDS TO FOLLOW HIS CHOSEN PATH.

ALONG THE WAY THERE ARE ALL TYPES OF SITUATIONS AND CIRCUMSTANCES THAT WILL STRENGTHEN HIS CHARACTER. THE BRAVE MAN'S DEDICATION AND COMMITMENT WILL BE TESTED. THROUGH THESE EXPERIENCES HE GAINS NEW WISDOM.

WHEN THE MOMENT OF TRUTH ARRIVES HE FEELS A CALM CONFIDENCE. HIS COURAGE IS PART OF HIS BEING. HE BRAVELY ADVANCES FORWARD STANDING IN HIS CHOSEN FIELD OF BATTLE. HIS ATTACKS ARE BOISTEROUS AND HEARTFELT. HE IS READY FOR THE ULTIMATE SACRIFICE.

HE MAY SUCCEED OR DIE TRYING. TO HIM THE RISK IS WORTH THE REWARD. HIS ACTIONS ARE JUSTIFIED. HE'S A HERO. HE HAS NO FEAR FOR HIS PERSONAL SAFETY. HE IS THE EPITOME OF SELFLESSNESS. THE GLORY OF HIS CAUSE CANNOT BE SURPASSED. HIS CHOSEN PATH IS NOT EASY ONE.

IT'S ALL ABOUT MORALE

Both winning and defeatist attitudes are contagious. Morale often makes the difference between victory and defeat. It is up to inspiring leaders to steer everything in the right direction. Through proper influences and positive motivation this can be done.

Maintaining morale can become a mental game of psychological warfare. All types of methods are used in an attempt to cause doubt and division. Masters of propaganda will spread lies to inspire fear which can have a disheartening effect. By adding small truths they attempt to add merit to their words. Wise men can see right through the sham and shine a light on these weak hearted tactics. Crushing these lame attempts show the power of morale.

Being highly organized and having discipline helps in all aspects and has many advantages. Knowing your organization's strengths and assets is a great way to prepare for any interactions that may occur. Having information on all the competition gives the knowledge and the know how that is needed to be ahead of the game. Being able to pick the other side's moves, well in advance is a sign of superiority, which does not go unnoticed.

The key to high morale comes from the roots of a strong company core. Like knights at the roundtable, the solidarity can be felt. Through heartfelt discussions our dreams and inspirations become reality.

Every elite company follows a strategy that is designed so that they can thrive and prosper. These game plans often have different stages set in place so achievements are more gratifying. Recognizing and striking down all the competition's ploys become an enjoyable pastime. With this general conception these potential threats get eliminated with new found efficiency. All victorious exchanges should be advertised for all to see.

Our minds and will must be strong. We must constantly reinforce what separates us from everyone else. Focus on areas of strength and it will show. By being on the same page no infection can penetrate our defenses. Division is one ploy that cannot enter our environment because simply put, it means destruction. Unity is the power that continues civilization with a momentous energy that makes everyone feel confident and secure. When an organization gets together and yells their company name, with unrestrained pride, morale becomes the triumphant theme and that's the way it supposed to be.

ONLY THE STRONG SURVIVE

WITHOUT ANY FORM OF STRENGTH, FAILURE, DEFEAT AND ANNIHILATION ARE A LIKELY FATE. STRENGTH HAS GREAT VALUE. IT CAN BE GAUGED BY THE MIND, BODY AND HEART THAT A LIVING SOUL POSSESSES.

BEING MENTALLY ACUTE IS THE KEY TO UTILIZING OUR STRENGTHS. THIS ALLOWS US TO FORM A SUPERIOR STRATEGY TO ENSURE SUCCESS. ACTING IN THIS FASHION WILL HELP US OBTAIN THE WEAPONS WE NEED FOR SURVIVAL.

AN INTELLIGENT BEING REALIZES THERE IS STRENGTH IN NUMBERS. UNIFYING STRONG FORCES WILL VALIDATE SUPERIORITY. THUS A NEW LEVEL OF STRENGTH CAN BE ACHIEVED.

A MAN WITH A STRONG MIND KNOWS HOW TO OVERCOME ADVERSITY. HE CANNOT BE SWAYED. NO MATTER WHAT THE CIRCUMSTANCES HE WILL STAY TRUE TO HIS BELIEFS.

STRENGTH OF BODY CAN BE MEASURED BY HOW PHYSICALLY STRONG A MAN IS AND BY HOW MUCH HE CAN ENDURE. STAY POWER, THE ABILITY TO OVERCOME PAIN, AND THE PURE RAW POWER THAT IS NEEDED TO PERFORM FEATS OF STRENGTH DESCRIBE THIS TYPE.

SOME BEINGS WILL NEVER BOW DOWN PHYSICALLY OR MENTALLY. THEY REFUSE TO GIVE UP. HOW THEY DEAL WITH DIFFICULTIES AND HARDSHIPS HELPS THEM CONTINUE TO SURVIVE.

MEN THAT SET HIGHER STANDARDS FOR THEMSELVES HAVE A FIRE BURNING WITHIN. THEIR FAITH IS A POWERFUL UNRELENTING FORCE. THIS TYPE OF MAN GAINS STRENGTH OF CHARACTER THROUGH HISACCOMPLISHMENTS. IN HIS PRESENCE A DISTINGUISHED AURA CAN BE FELT.

MEN THAT HARBOR STRENGTH HAVE AN IRON WILL. THEY WILL ALWAYS GIVE THE EXTRA THAT IS NEEDED TO OVERCOME WHAT EVER OBSTACLES LIFE PUTS IN FRONT OF THEM. THUS ONLY THE STRONG WILL SURVIVE.

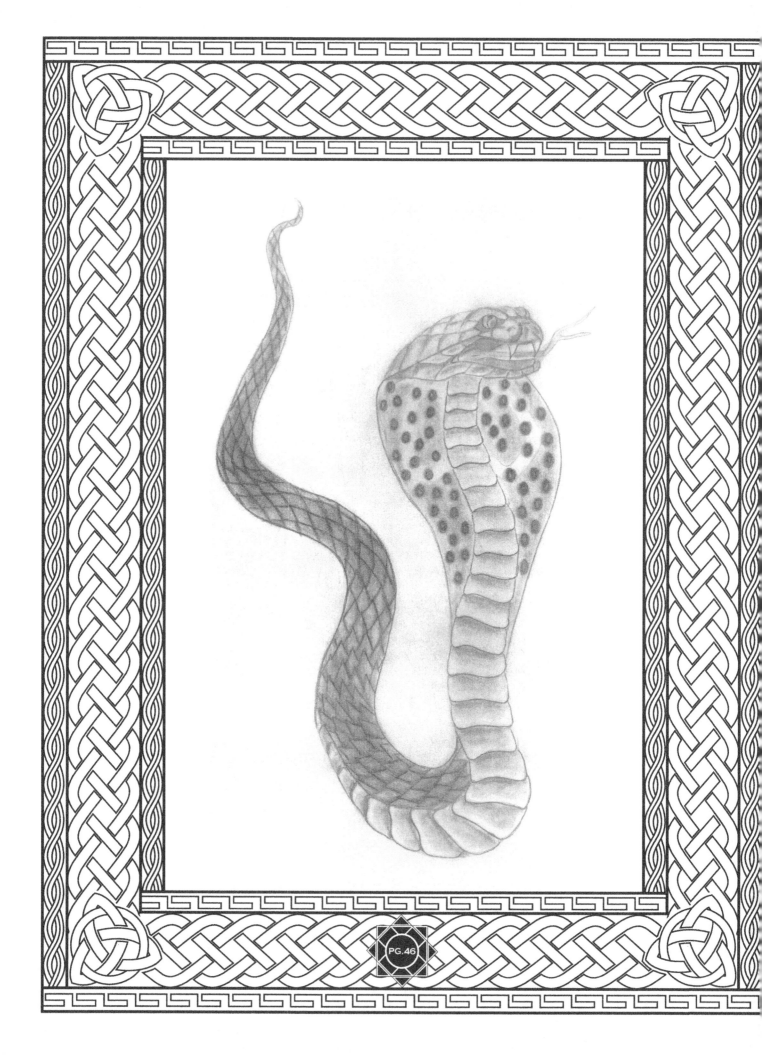

WORTHY POSSESSIONS

WHEN WE MAKE IMPORTANT DECISIONS WE MAKE THEM BASED ON WHETHER WE BELIEVE OUR CHOICE TO BE WORTH IT. NOT ALL PEOPLE VALUE THE SAME THINGS. SOME CRAVE WEALTH AND POWER WHILE OTHERS DESIRE HAPPINESS AND FULFILMENT. AS MEN WE VALUE MANY THINGS. THERE IS A LOT OF DEPTH TO THESE VALUES MAKING THEM POTENTIALLY DIFFERENT WITH EACH CIRCUMSTANCE.

WE LIVE OUR LIFE BASED ON WHAT WE DESIRE. THE PRINCIPLES WE LIVE BY INFLUENCE WHAT WE VALUE MOST. MOST PEOPLE CHERISH LOVE AND PEACE. OUR WIVES AND CHILDREN BECOME PART OF OUR LIFE, FILLING US FULL OF LOVE AND JOY, MAKING US FEEL COMPLETE. OUR LOVE FOR THEM INSPIRES US TO MAKE A GOOD LIVING SO WE CAN SHOWER THEM WITH GIFTS OF AFFECTION AND HELP FUND THEIR LIFE'S VENTURES.

THE DIRECTION OF OUR LIFE'S FLOW OFTEN FEELS FULL OF PURPOSE. EMBRACING THIS CALLING CAN BE A VERY SATISFYING EXPERIENCE. ONE MAY REALIZE THAT HE IS THE ONLY PERSON IN THE WORLD THAT CAN COMPLETE THIS TASK, WHICH GIVES HIM A SENSE OF WORTH. FOLLOWING A PATH FULL OF DEVOTION MAKES OBTAINING OUR GOAL MORE REWARDING AND ACHIEVEMENTS MORE SATISFYING. A CONTINUATION OF OUR LIFE'S WORK LONG AFTER WE ARE GONE IS A MOTIVATIONAL CONCEPT.

SOME PEOPLE LIVE TO SEE PEACE AND HARMONY IN THE WORLD. THEY STRIVE TO HELP OTHERS. THEY FEEL A GREAT JOY WHEN THEY LIFT SOMEONE'S SPIRITS. THEY DEVOTE THEIR TIME TO SUPPORTING AND ENLIGHTENING PEOPLE. THEY DESIRE TO INSPIRE HOPE AND GIVE STRENGTH TO INDIVIDUALS THAT ARE IN NEED. TO THEM THIS IS A MEANINGFUL REWARDING EXPERIENCE. THE HAPPINESS THEY POSSESS IN THEIR HEARTS IS ALL THEY NEED.

THERE ARE MEN THAT DO NOT SEE PAST THEIR OWN DESIRES. THEY ONLY CARE ABOUT PHYSICAL POSSESSIONS AND BEING ABLE TO USE THEIR ASSETS TO CONTROL WHATEVER THEY CAN. THEY ARE ONLY AFTER POWER. HOW THEIR ACTIONS AFFECT OTHERS IS NOT THEIR CONCERN. TO THEM THE ULTIMATE REWARD IS HAVING UNLIMITED AMOUNTS OF MONEY AND POWER SO THEY CAN BEND PEOPLES WILL. EVERY TIME SOMEONE THROWS AWAY THEIR MORALS IN EXCHANGE FOR A PROFIT THESE INDIVIDUALS FEEL A SENSE OF TRIUMPH.

SOME PEOPLE ARE MORE CONCERNED ABOUT PHYSICAL POSSESSIONS BUT OTHERS ARE CONTENT WITH WHAT'S IN THEIR HEARTS. IN PARTS OF THE WORLD A SNAKE IS CONSIDERED A SYMBOL OF WEALTH. A SNAKE IS VIEWED IN MANY WAYS. LETTING OUR CRAVINGS FOR VALUABLE POSSESSIONS DETERMINE OUR PATH WOULD GRANT THE MOST NEGATIVE VIEW. THEREFORE WE MUST MAINTAIN A BALANCE. WE CAN BE THE MASTER OF THE SERPENT RATHER THAN LETTING THE SERPENT DICTATE WHAT WE CHOOSE TO DESIRE. WHEN WE PASS ON WE CANNOT TAKE ANYTHING WITH US, ONLY OUR LEGACY REMAINS. LEAVING OUR LOVED ONES ALL OF THE BELONGINGS WE HAVE ACQUIRED THROUGH OUR LIFE IS REWARDING BECAUSE WE WANT TO SHARE OUR LIFE'S WORK WITH THEM AND GIVE THEM ONE LAST GIFT FROM OUR HEARTS.

WITH A CLEAR UNDERSTANDING OF WHAT INSPIRES US, WE REALIZE LIFE ISN'T ABOUT THE NUMBER OF BREATHS WE TAKE BUT RATHER THE GRATIFYING MOMENTS THAT TAKE OUR BREATH AWAY. WHAT WE POSSESS IN OUR HEARTS IS THERE TO STAY.

BONAFIDE PRIDE

PEOPLE ARE PROUD OF MANY THINGS. A MAN MAY BE PROUD OF HIS SUCCESS OR THE ACCOMPLISHMENTS OF THOSE HE HOLDS IN HIGH REGARD. NO MATTER WHAT THE CASE PRIDE GIVES US A TRIUMPHANT FEELING.

AS MEN WE TAKE PRIDE IN A WIDE RANGE OF ACHIEVEMENTS. BEING ENTRUSTED WITH IMPORTANT INFORMATION, HAVING THE HIGHEST STANDARDS, AND EMERGING VICTORIOUS FROM ANY ONE OF LIFE'S CHALLENGES INDULGE US WITH PRIDE.

TOO MUCH OF ANYTHING CAN HAVE NEGATIVE EFFECTS. HAVING TOO BIG OF AN EGO CAN MAKE US UNREASONABLE AND BLIND TO THE TRUTH. BY NOT ACTING WITH HUMILITY WE BECOME TOO PROUD TO ADMIT ANY SETBACKS OR WRONGDOING. THIS OBSTINATE ATTITUDE CAN RESULT IN POOR DECISIONS BEING MADE. THIS TYPE OF COCKY AMBITION CAN BE DISASTROUS.

THERE IS NOTHING WRONG WITH BEING ENTHUSIASTIC, HAPPY, OR SATISFIED. WHETHER IT IS OUR LOVED ONE'S SUCCESS OR OUR OWN IT FEELS GREAT TO CELEBRATE. TAKING PRIDE IN ANYTHING WE LOVE AND SUPPORT MAKES US FEEL RIGHTEOUSLY REWARDED. THE POWER OF POSITIVE ENERGY IS AWESOME AND MANIFESTS UNINHIBITED FEELINGS OF GRANDEUR.

PRIDE CAN PRODUCE A GLORIOUS FEELING, LIKE STANDING ON THE VERY TOP OF THE MOUNTAIN, CELEBRATING AN UNIMAGINABLE VICTORY. THE RUSH OF ADRENALINE MAKES US CONFIDENT AND PROUD THAT ANYONE PRESENT CAN FEEL THE AURA, ADDING ALL THE MORE TO THE EXCITEMENT OF IT.

WE MUST BE MINDFUL OF THOSE THAT FEEL THREATENED OR TAKE OFFENSE TO OUR EXAGGERATED EXPRESSIONS. THEY MAY WISH TO TARNISH AND TAKE OUR ENJOYMENT AWAY. CONTAINING OUR JOY MAY FEEL IMPOSSIBLE HOWEVER A HUMBLE DIGNIFIED APPROACH IS BY FAR THE BEST COURSE OF ACTION. BONAFIDE PRIDE IS HARD TO HIDE. SO WE CAN EMBRACE IT AND LET THE ENERGY ENGULF OUR INNER BEING SO WITH EACH BREATH THE POWER CAN BE FELT WITHOUT A SINGLE WORD BEING SAID.

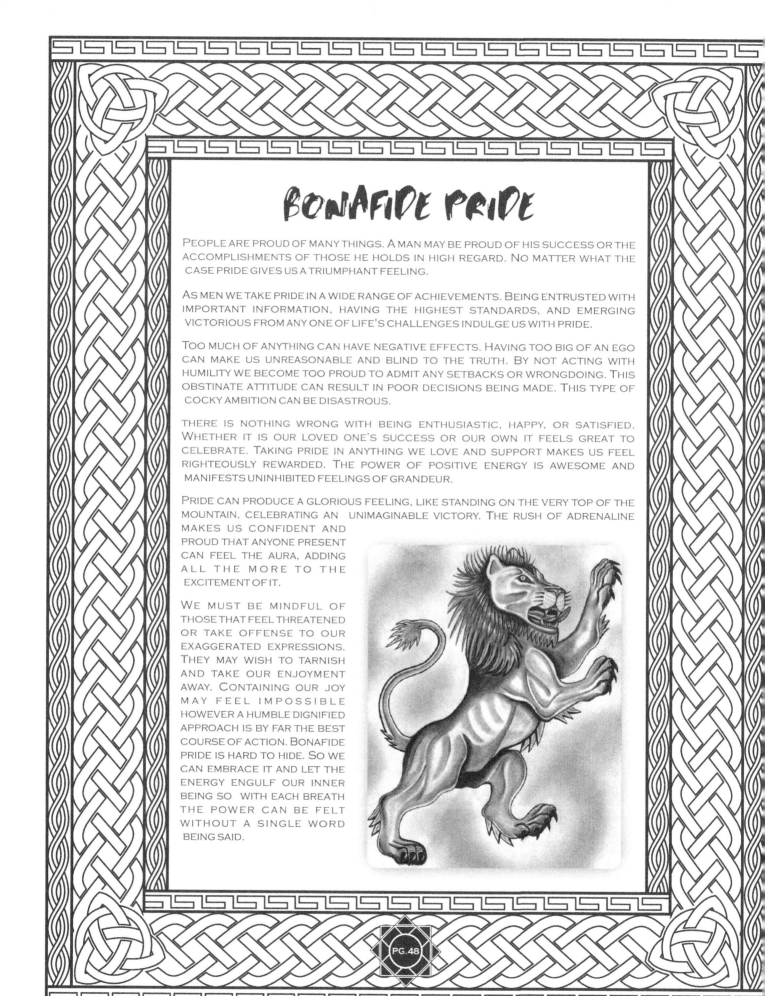

UNIVERSAL HARMONY

IN A REALM WHERE THERE IS NO FEAR, PEACE AND HAPPINESS THRIVE. CLEAN AIR, FRESHWATER, AND FOOD OF SUBSTANCE SPAWN A HEALTHY MIND AND BODY. THESE ELEMENTS ARE THE KEYS FOR LONGEVITY. TOGETHER THEY CREATE AN ENVIRONMENT FULL OF BLISS WITH CLARITY, UNITY, AND PURPOSE. EVERYTHING HAS A PLACE. AS THE SEASONS TRANSFORM FROM THE SUN, TO THE RAIN, TO THE SNOW THERE IS A CONSTANT FLOW. THE CLOUDS IN THE SKY, THE MOUNTAINS WITH THE TREES, THE AIR WITH A BREEZE. THERE IS A REALIZATION THAT HEAVEN AND EARTH ARE THE COMBINED FORCE THAT BALANCES NATURE. WITH THE RIGHT VIEW A WONDERFUL WISDOM IS ACHIEVED. THIS BRINGS FORWARD ACCEPTANCE SO THAT ALL NEGATIVE THOUGHTS AND ENERGY CAN NO LONGER EXIST. A RELAXING TRANQUIL SETTING IS LIKE FLOWERS WHEN THEY BLOOM. THE FEELING OF FREEDOM IS LIKE A BIRD FLYING THROUGH THE SKY. THE ATMOSPHERE CREATES A JOY THAT GUIDES US TO BE LOVING, GIVING, AND COMPASSIONATE. ONCE THIS ENLIGHTENMENT IS ACHIEVED EACH BREATH, EACH MEAL, AND EVERY THOUGHT IS IN COMPLETE HARMONY WITH THE UNIVERSE.

Harmony

Hachiman

A BATTLE WORTH FIGHTING

WHY MUST MEN WAR?. RELIGION, SELF-PRESERVATION, AND CONTROL ARE THE COMMON REASONS. WOUNDED PRIDE, JEALOUSY, AND THE THIRST FOR POWER WILL CAUSE WAR. MEN WILL KILL FOR KNOWLEDGE OR TO STOP OTHERS FROM OBTAINING IT. IN THE NAME OF RELIGION THERE IS A POWERFUL UNITY. IN THIS MATTER, PEOPLE'S MINDS CAN BE MANIPULATED VERY EASILY. DEFENDING ONE'S HOMELAND IS HONORABLE. WHEN RELIGION IS USED AS A TOOL TO TAKE AND CONQUER IT BECOMES EVIL. RELIGION IS FOR DOING GOOD NOT CAUSING DEATH OR DESTRUCTION. IN THIS WORLD THERE ARE OPPRESSOR'S. SOME WARS ARE FOUGHT FOR FREEDOM. DEFIANT PEOPLE WOULD RATHER FIGHT THAN BE SUBMISSIVE. THIS CREATES A REBELLION. AS HISTORY CLEARLY STATES REBELS ARE OFTEN SUCCESSFUL BECAUSE THEY STRONGLY BELIEVE IN THE CAUSE THEY'RE FIGHTING FOR. ENEMIES OF REBELS ARE CONSTANTLY TRYING TO LOOK FOR THEM BUT NEVER SEE THEM. THEY TRY TO LISTEN FOR THEM BUT HEAR ALL THE WRONG THINGS. THEY TRY TO LOCATE THEM BUT NEVER SEEM TO FIND THEM. THIS IS THE WAY OF THE FREEDOM FIGHTER. THIS TYPE OF WAR IS NOT BY CHOICE. THEY SAY ALL IS FAIR IN LOVE AND WAR. A MAN MUST DO EVERYTHING IN HIS POWER TO PROTECT HIS LOVED ONES AND HIS COUNTRY.

OTHERS ABUSE SITUATIONS. THEY FABRICATE AND INSTIGATE SO THAT THEY CAN TAKE WHAT DOES NOT BELONG TO THEM. THEY CREATE AN ILLUSION TO MAKE IT LOOK LIKE THEY ARE HELPING RATHER THAN HURTING. BEWARE OF FALSE PROPAGANDA. THESE MEN DESIRE GREAT WEALTH AND POWER, SO THEY EASILY LIE AND MANIPULATE TO GET THEIR WAY.

WITH THIS BEING SAID A MAN MUST NEVER COMMIT TO ANYTHING UNLESS HE KNOWS ALL THE FACTS TO BE TRUE. ALWAYS SEE THINGS FOR WHAT THEY ARE, DON'T BE BLINDED BY THE PROMISE OF GREAT REWARDS. DON'T GIVE THE OTHER SIDE FUEL FOR THEIR FIRE, LET SILENCE BE YOUR WEAPON. ONCE YOU HAVE COMMITTED TO A COURSE OF ACTION THERE'S NO TURNING BACK. EMOTION CAN BE THE ENEMY, DON'T LET THE WRONG STATE OF MIND MAKE YOUR DECISIONS.

WHY ARE SOME MEN BLINDED BY AMBITION? THEY THINK ALL THEIR ACTIONS ARE JUSTIFIED. THEY TRULY BELIEVE THEY CANNOT BE DEFEATED. NO ONE IS ABOVE EVENTUAL DEFEAT. EVERYTHING ALWAYS COMES FULL CIRCLE. THERE WILL ALWAYS BE RETRIBUTION.

WHY DO THE POOR FIGHT THE DICTATORS WAR? WHY DON'T THE RICH THAT MAKE THE LAWS HAVE THEIR CHILDREN ENLIST IN THE BATTLE THEY CLAIM THEY SO STRONGLY SUPPORT. THE ANSWER IS SIMPLE: LEAVE THE JOB TO THE PAWNS THAT DON'T KNOW BETTER. HOW DO WE PRESERVE THE PEACE? MANY THINGS CAN DISRUPT HARMONY. BUT WE MUST TRY TO FIND A BALANCE. FINDING A COMPROMISE MAY BE NEXT TO IMPOSSIBLE. MANY PEOPLE CONFUSE KINDNESS FOR WEAKNESS. WHEN ALL ELSE FAILS WE TRY TO JUSTIFY OUR COURSE OF ACTION. BY FORCE OR BY REASON BECOMES THE REAL LIFE GAME OF CHESS.

IN THIS STRUGGLE THEY SAY KEEP YOUR FRIENDS CLOSE YOUR ENEMIES CLOSER. BEWARE OF THE TIGER ACTING LIKE HE DOESN'T DESIRE FLESH. DIVIDING A NATION AND CONQUERING IT HAS BEEN A SUCCESSFUL STRATEGY THAT HAS WITHSTOOD THE TEST OF TIME. HOWEVER MEN THAT STAND UNITED FOR THE GOOD OF THEIR PEOPLE HAVE ALWAYS PREVAILED ABOVE ALL ELSE.

WE MUST THINK, FEEL, AND SEE HOW THE OTHER SIDE VIEWS THINGS. TRY WALKING IN THEIR SHOES. WE MUST KNOW WHEN TO STOP DON'T LET THAT THIRST FOR BATTLE CONTINUE ONCE THE OBJECTIVE HAS BEEN ACHIEVED. WHAT WAS ONCE GOOD WILL BECOME A FORCE OF EVIL.

SOME MEN ARE TRUTHFUL, WHILE OTHERS DECEIVE. SOME MEN SHOW COURAGE WHILE OTHERS ARE COWARDS. IN THE END SOME GAIN GLORY, OTHERS SADNESS. RUTHLESSNESS IS COMMON WHERE MERCY IS RARE. WAR CAN BRING OUT THE BEST AND WORST IN PEOPLE. IT CAN AFFECT HOW MANY GENERATIONS COME TO VIEW THINGS, WHICH CAN CREATE A BIAS AND DESTROY ANY FUTURE HOPES OF PEACE. FOR EVERY CAUSE THERE IS AN EFFECT. BEING TRIUMPHANT IN A BATTLE IS GREAT, BUT THAT DOES NOT ENSURE WINNING THE WAR. ONE MUST THINK LONG TERM AND IF THE BATTLE IS REALLY WORTH FIGHTING. IN WAR THE BEST VICTORY IS A BATTLE NOT EVEN FOUGHT.

Mao Zedong

STANDING STRONG

There comes a time when continuous failure can no longer be tolerated. Being considered primitive, low class, and weak is not acceptable. This is what motivates people to set higher standards for themselves. To bring forth this type of change is not easy. Throughout history great leaders have always found a way to get people to work towards a common goal. These type of men have opened peoples eyes so they can see and feel the power of unity.

At one point in history the Mongols often fell victim. When the legendary Genghis Khan was a child his mother taught him about strength and unity. She gave him an arrow and told him to break it. He bent the arrow and broke it. She then told him to grab a bunch of arrows and try breaking them all at once. He could not break the arrows. He learned that when people stand together they become much stronger. He had no bias towards other races or customs. His focus was on unity and strength. With all his soldiers loyal and disciplined he was content. He understood what his mother taught him very well. He became one of the most successful leaders in history of the world.

The great Chinese leader Mao Zedong preached to his people about what China needed to do to become respected. After the brutal Japanese occupation of China his people could relate to his words of passion. He had a fanatical determination to make China strong no matter what the cost. There was much suffering and self-sacrifice. He made the Chinese people proud and brought forth their fighting spirit. The Korean War was a classic example of how Mao united the people of China. He obtained his goal when China developed nuclear weapons. Today China is a major superpower. Every patriotic person in China pays homage to Mao Zedong. They praise what he did for his people.

During the British occupation of India unjust taxes were placed upon the people of India. There was one man who stood strong, united the people, and changed India forever, his name is Mahatma Gandhi. He emulated the power of unity by leading massive peaceful protests for a cause he believed in. Gandhi lead by example and was willing to suffer for what he believed was right. He believed in treating everyone equal regardless of cast or religion. Martin Luther King later mirrored these same principles to demand equality for the black people of America. No threat of force or violence could defeat Gandhi's nonviolent approach to achieving equality and fairness. India eventually obtained complete independence. Gandhi proved that large-scale nonviolent peaceful protests are the most powerful form of unity known to man. Through his teachings we learned that when people are willing to put personal feelings aside and stand side-by-side for a worthy cause, as a whole everyone can thrive. Gandhi was a hero.

A great leader has a fire burning within. His source of passion can inflame anyone that it touches, thus inspiring people to stand together for a righteous cause. By embracing the ideals of a worthy leader people find both clarity and purpose.

Certain principles must be followed so that people can stand strong. First they must share a common goal and be passionate about it. Furthermore a strong support network is necessary. Also people must be willing to help each other mentally as well as physically. This requires a mutual effort from everyone involved. When people know they are not alone they gain a powerful sense of purpose. This type of help and support makes all the difference.

Doubt causes division and separates people. It is a poison that can cause mass destruction. Selflessness unites people. It is the ultimate cure, it can unite strangers and families alike. Through realization and commitment we can harness a power never thought possible. United we stand, divided we fall. There is only one logical choice. As individuals we must find a way to stand together so we can truly understand what we are capable of.

不屈

The Monkey King

THE INDOMITABLE SPIRIT OF A WARRIOR

SOME MEN HAVE THE ABILITY TO KEEP GOING ON REGARDLESS OF HOW GRIM THE FUTURE LOOKS. NO MATTER HOW MANY TIMES THEY GET KNOCKED DOWN THEY WILL KEEP GETTING UP.

THIS TYPE OF MAN IS NO ORDINARY INDIVIDUAL. HIS MIND, BODY, AND SPIRIT ARE IN UNISON. HE IS LIKE A MOTIVATED MACHINE THAT DOESN'T SEE QUITTING AS AN OPTION. THE DECISION HAS BEEN MADE. HE WILL KEEP MARCHING FORWARD. THE FIGHT WILL CONTINUE.

HE HAS NO PLACE FOR NEGATIVE THOUGHTS. THE FORCE WITHIN HIM BOLDLY DEALS WITH EVERY OBSTACLE THAT COMES BEFORE HIM. THERE IS NO EXCUSE FOR BEING DISHEARTENED. HE CAN ALWAYS SEE THE CHANCE FOR SUCCESS.

IN A PHYSICAL SITUATION THAT SEVERELY LIMITS HIS OPTIONS, HIS MIND REMAINS STRONG. HE WILL LET THE ENEMY FEEL HIS RETREAT AND DEFEAT. BUT HE IS SIMPLY CALCULATING AND BUYING TIME FOR THE ONE CHANCE HE NEEDS. HIS FOCUS IS OVERWHELMINGLY POWERFUL.

HE IS A CONSTANT THREAT TO THOSE WHO OPPOSE HIM BECAUSE HE WILL NEVER BOW DOWN OR ACCEPT DEFEAT. HIS DEDICATION IS DANGEROUS. HE IS LIKE A PREDATOR THAT IS ALWAYS READY TO STRIKE WHEN EVER A MISTAKE IS MADE.

HE WILL NEVER GIVE UP HOPE, NEVER STOP FIGHTING, AND NEVER STOP LOOKING FOR THE OPPORTUNITY HE NEEDS TO PREVAIL. IT IS HIS DUTY TO THRIVE. THE INDOMITABLE SPIRIT OF A WARRIOR IS IMPOSSIBLE TO SUBMIT.

THE RIGHT TO DEFEND

In a life that is content one grows to love his family, his homeland, his livelihood, and his good name. When any of this becomes hurt or threatened one must Man up and defend all that he holds dear. We must defend our freedom and Quality of life.

In a righteous state of mind we feel compassion which obligates us to protect the innocent and helpless. We despise all the predators that prey upon those we feel duty bound to protect. Thus we have the ability to transform into the predator of predators. With our senses heightened our instincts thrive to destroy the threat that presents itself.

Even a lesser man will surprise himself with the fire that burns inside him when his children are threatened. A power is formed that greatly surpasses the norm. We cherish the good lives our loved ones live. It becomes our responsibility to defend it. As men we know when it's time to fight. We must remove the cancer that threatens our existence. We must guard our reputation against insults. Negative propaganda can create more enemies and shift the tide in favour of the other side. Our actions must be concise and bold so we can stop this from happening and maintain balance.

If someone attacks us we must repel them and eliminate the threat. Our livelihood is an important part of our life we cannot let anyone take it away, it is the power behind our success and harmony.

We are selfish and unwise if we do not constantly train and prepare for the threats that can arise. When the enemy sees a strong Defense they are less motivated to invade our territory. Let this be the ultimate motivation to make it of the highest caliber. Never become too relaxed or confident. Be sure and alert. Nothing is guaranteed in life. When a situation arrives we must be ready and willing to defend against all tyrants otherwise everything we love will be destroyed.

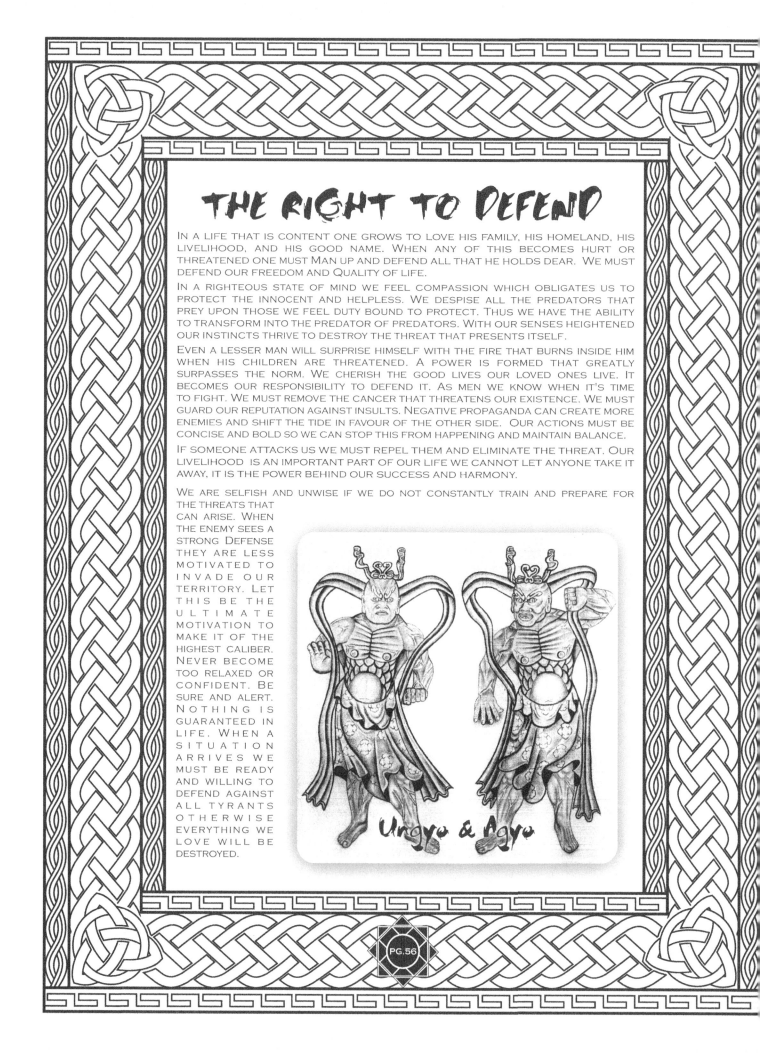

Ungyo & Agyo

WHEN FIGHTING SPIRITS THRIVE

FOR SOME COMBAT OR ANY TYPE OF CONFRONTATIONAL SITUATION IS ONE THEY WILL TRY TO AVOID. WHILE OTHERS LOVE THE CHALLENGE AND EMBRACE IT WITH ENTHUSIASM.

WARRIORS WILLING TO ACCEPT A CHALLENGE PROJECT A STRONG AURA. PEOPLE RESPECT AND FEAR THESE TYPES OF MEN. THEY ARE A FORCE TO RECKON WITH THAT HAVE A FEARLESS FIRE IN THEIR EYES. THEIR CONFIDENCE AND INTENSITY IS A PROMINENT ENERGY THAT CAN BE FELT TO THE CORE. THEY DO NOT LOOK PAST WHAT STANDS BEFORE THEM. THEY PUT IT ALL ON THE LINE AND FOCUS ON THE TASK AT HAND. THEY ACCEPT ALL CHALLENGES, NEVER TAKING THE EASY WAY OUT.

IN DEFEAT THEY CAN'T WAIT FOR A REMATCH OR A CHANCE TO REDEEM THEMSELVES. THEY LEARN FROM THEIR MISTAKES AND USE THEIR NEW FOUND KNOWLEDGE TO ATTACK WITH VIGOR. WHEN OTHERS THINK THEY CAN'T WIN THEY WILL DO EVERYTHING IN THEIR POWER TO PROVE THEY CAN. THEY HAVE AN OVERWHELMING URGE TO KNOCK ALL RIVALS DOWN TO SIZE. WHEN THESE WARRIORS FEEL ANY DOUBT OR CONCERN THEY WILL FACE THESE ISSUES IMMEDIATELY BECAUSE TO THEM THIS IS A TEST OF THEIR INTEGRITY. THEY WILL NOT SHIRK AWAY FROM ANY CHALLENGE.

JUST LIKE FAMOUS REVOLUTIONARIES OF THE PAST THESE INDIVIDUALS WOULD RATHER DIE ON THEIR FEET, FIGHTING, THAN LIVE A LIFE OF SERVITUDE, ON THEIR KNEES, TO SOMEONE THEY FEEL IS DOING THEM WRONG. THEY WANT TO FIGHT FOR WHAT THEY BELIEVE IN. THEY ARE WILLING TO CONFRONT ALL THEIR FEARS TO OBTAIN THE ULTIMATE REWARD "VICTORY". TO THEM THE RISK IS WORTH THE REWARD. DEEP DOWN, THEY KNOW THEY MUST WANT IT MORE AND TRY HARDER, NO EFFORT NOT BEING THEIR ALL. WHEN EVERYTHING BECOMES DIFFICULT THROUGH SHALLOW BREATHING AND FATIGUE THEIR WILL DRIVES THEM NOT JUST TO ENDURE, BUT TO PREVAIL. THE THRILL OF COMBAT AND THEIR DESIRE TO ACHIEVE THEIR GOALS GIVES THEM THE RUSH THEY NEED TO PUSH THE LIMIT. THUS THEIR FIGHTING SPIRITS THRIVE.

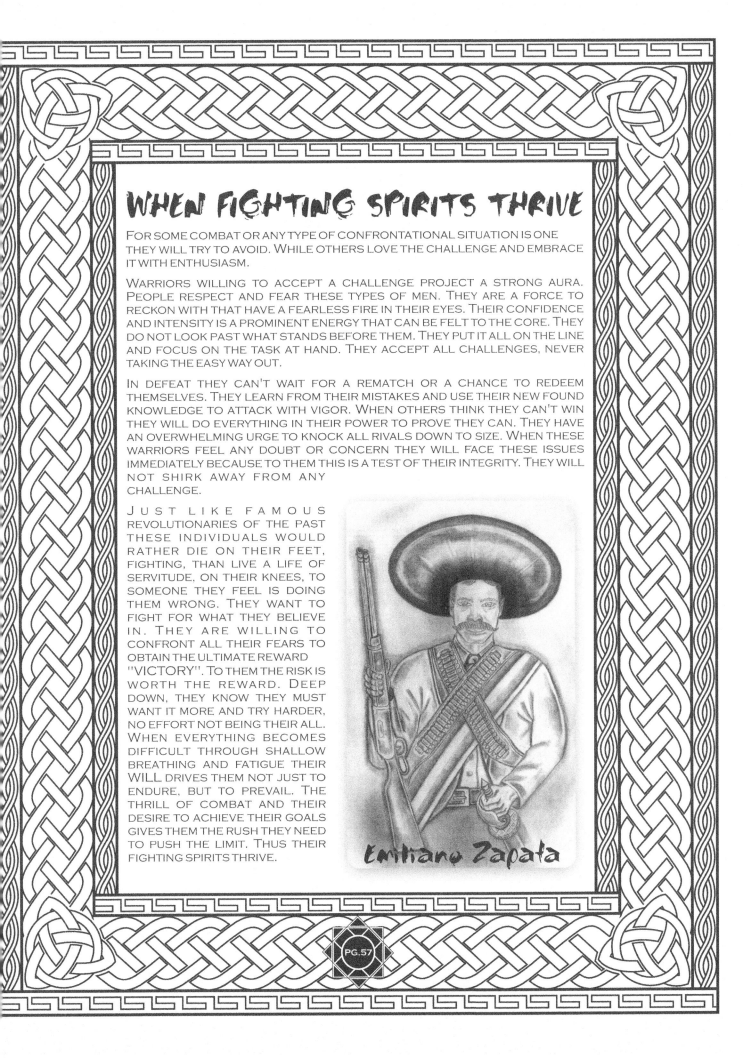

Emiliano Zapata

TO STRIKE WITH VENGEANCE

SOMETIMES A SITUATION ARISES WHEN ABUSE CAN NO LONGER BE TOLERATED. WHEN A PEACEFUL LIFE IS DEVASTATED. ALL OPTIONS ARE TERMINATED. PAIN, BETRAYAL, AND EMPTINESS CANNOT BE IGNORED. WHEN A MAN'S FAMILY AND LOVED ONES ARE KILLED OR VIOLATED THE LINE HAS BEEN CROSSED. WHEN OUR HOMELAND'S RAVAGED AND OUR LIVELIHOOD'S DESTROYED WE HAVE NOTHING LEFT TO DO, BUT SEEK VENGEANCE. WHEN THE INNOCENT FALL, VICTIM WE CAN NO LONGER TURN THE OTHER CHEEK.

MANY QUESTIONS COME TO ONE'S MIND. WHY DID THIS HAPPEN? WHY DID THEY DO THIS? COULD THIS HAVE BEEN AVOIDED? NOW WE ARE FORCED TO REACT.

THERE IS A HORRIBLE AGONIZING FEELING IN THE PIT OF A MAN'S STOMACH. HE FEELS HATE, ANGER, AND RAGE. OUR SUFFERING AND SENSE OF LOSS MAKES US WANT TO PUNISH EVERYTHING AND EVERYONE THAT CAUSED OUR PAIN. WE WANT TO LASH OUT. THE EMOTION WE FEEL FUELS A RUTHLESS NEED FOR REVENGE.

THEY SAY THE BEST DEFENSE IS OFFENSE. SOME MEN WILL BLAME THEMSELVES FOR NOT BEING ABLE TO STOP AN ENEMY ATTACK. THEY WILL MAKE SEEKING RETRIBUTION THEIR SOLE MISSION IN LIFE. A CALMNESS IS NEEDED SO THE ATTACK IS INITIATED PROPERLY. THERE IS ONLY ONE CHANCE TO GET IT RIGHT. A SMART MAN WILL MAKE THE ENEMY FEEL THAT HE HAS GIVEN UP AND SEEKS ONLY PEACE. THE ELEMENT OF SURPRISE IS A POWERFUL WEAPON. THE ATTACKS CAUSE MAYHEM, CHAOS, AND DESTRUCTION. THE OTHER SIDE NOW FEELS THE SAME PAIN. IT'S PAYBACK TIME. THEIR PUNISHMENT IS CARRIED OUT WITH THE UTMOST DETERMINATION. SUFFERING IS RAMPANT. REVENGE FEELS SWEET.

WHEN THE DUST SETTLES, PEACE IS LOST AND PAIN IS FELT ON BOTH SIDES. THUS ELITE WARRIORS WILL BE SPAWNED FOR MANY MORE GENERATIONS TO COME. THIS BECOMES A CYCLE OF VENGEANCE. THERE IS ONLY TEMPORARY SATISFACTION. THE DAMAGE IS DONE. THERE ARE PERMANENT SCARS AND NOTHING CAN REPLACE THE SENSE OF LOSS. YET SOMETIMES A MAN MUST FIGHT FOR WHAT'S RIGHT. ONCE A DRAGON IS AWAKENED THERE WILL BE AN UN-RESTRAINED WRATH WITH NO LETTING UP. EVERY NATION HAS A DRAGON WITHIN. WE MUST DO OUR BEST TO MAINTAIN THE PEACE AND LET EVERY DRAGON ENJOY IT'S SLEEP.

OVERCOMING ORDEALS

SOMETIMES IN LIFE WE ENCOUNTER DISHEARTENING SITUATIONS. THESE ENCOUNTERS CAN FOREVER ALTER HOW WE REACT TO EVENTS IN THE FUTURE. A PERMANENT SCAR CAN BE FORMED. OUR MIND SET IS THE ONLY PHENOMENA THAT CAN GUIDE US TO OVERCOME THESE TURMOILS.

WAR, DEFEAT, INJURIES, BREAKUPS, DRUG ADDICTION, ABUSE, OR THE DEATH OF SOMEONE WE HOLD DEAR ARE EXAMPLES OF EVENTS THAT CAN CAUSE US PAIN AND TARNISH OUR INNER SOULS. HABITS WE DEVELOP CAN FUEL OUR CRAVING FOR ATTACHMENTS. ONLY PEACE WITHIN US CAN REPLACE ALL THAT WE ARE LACKING. IN THIS TYPE OF ENVIRONMENT, SUPPORT FROM OTHERS CAN BE VERY SOOTHING. HOWEVER, WE CAN NOT RELY ON OTHERS FOR PROTECTION. OUR INNER STRENGTH IS OUR TRUE SHIELD.

VICTORY OVER ONESELF IS OUR PRIMARY GOAL WHEN RECOVERING FROM TURMOIL. IT IS THIS ATTITUDE THAT ALLOWS US TO FOCUS ON A POSITIVE OUTCOME RATHER THAN A NEGATIVE EXPERIENCE. WE MUST NOT LET OUR HEARTS WAIVER, UNITY OF THE MIND IS ESSENTIAL AND PROVIDES THE STRENGTH WE NEED TO OVERCOME ADVERSITY. OUR MINDFUL AWARENESS SHINES A LIGHT ON EACH OBSTACLE WE FACE. THROUGH THESE ENCOUNTERS WE GAIN MORE KNOWLEDGE. THIS NEW FOUND WISDOM GIVES US THE CONFIDENCE WE NEED TO LEARN FROM EACH SETBACK AND PREVAIL OVER FUTURE ENDEAVOURS.

VIEWING THE WORLD WITHOUT FEAR OR LOATHING MAKES IT EASIER FOR US TO SAFELY OVERCOME ANY CRISIS THAT CONFRONTS US. HAVING A CALMNESS WITHIN GIVES US STRENGTH. WE LEARN FROM OUR EXPERIENCES, FAILURE SPAWNS SUCCESS. FROM EACH LESSON IN LIFE WE ARE TAUGHT SOMETHING NEW.

LIFE IS FULL OF TRIALS BUT OVERCOMING THEM MAKES THE MAN. THIS GIVES US A NEW LEASE ON LIFE. WE MUST BE GRATEFUL FOR ALL THE NEGATIVE PEOPLE, HARDSHIPS, AND SETBACKS BECAUSE THEY GIVE US AN OPPORTUNITY TO GROW AND REACH NEW LEVELS OF AWARENESS. EACH ORDEAL WE OVERCOME MAKES US STRONGER.

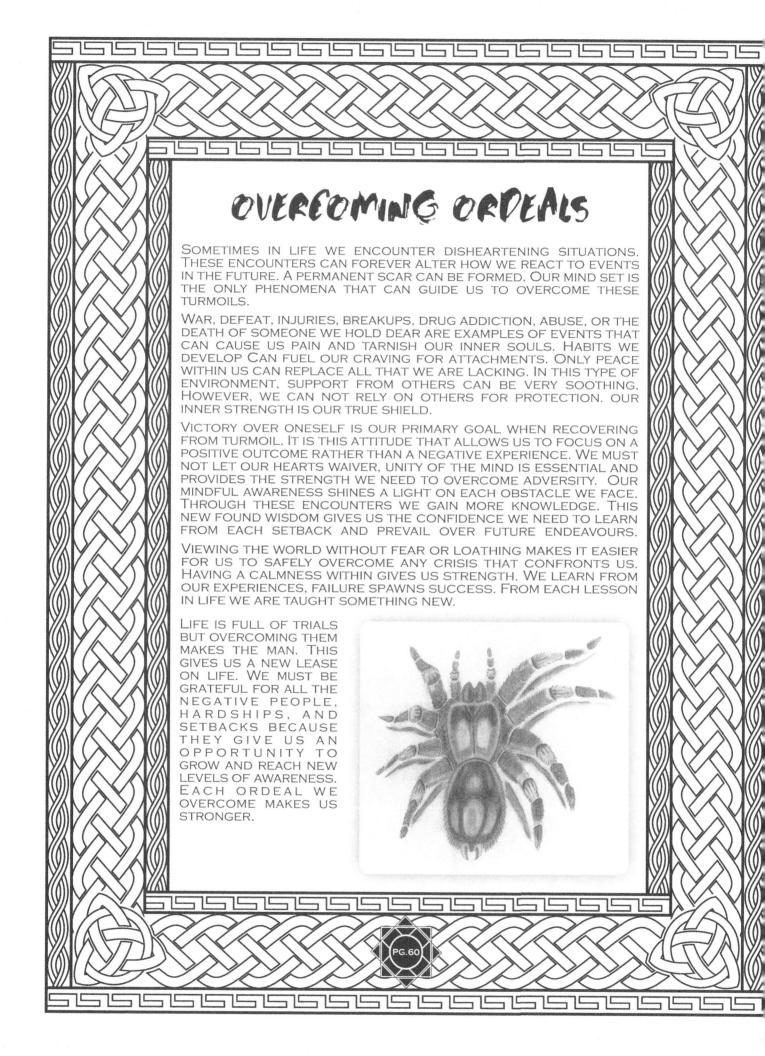

KARMIC FORMATIONS

HOW WE VIEW THINGS, WHAT WE INTEND TO DO, WHAT WE DO, WHAT WE SAY, HOW WE LIVE, HOW MUCH WE DEDICATE, HOW SHARP OUR FOCUS IS, AND HOW MINDFUL WE ARE OF OUR SURROUNDINGS WILL FORM OUR KARMA.

KARMIC FORMATIONS WAS, IS, AND ALWAYS WILL BE PART OF AN ONGOING CYCLE. IT IS UP TO EACH LIVING SOUL TO IMPROVE THEIR KARMA. EVERY ACTION HAS A REACTION. COWARDICE AND SELFISHNESS FORM A NEGATIVE. THE FEARLESS AND GIVING FORM A POSITIVE. GIVING, HELPING, AND DOING GOOD DEEDS WILL IMPROVE KARMA. TAKING, HARMING, AND AVOIDING THOSE IN NEED WILL ERODE GOOD KARMA. KNOW THERE IS A PRICE TO PAY FOR EVERYTHING DONE WITH OUT THE RIGHT INTENTIONS. SOMETIMES WE ARE WILLING TO PAY THE PRICE BECAUSE WE FEEL OBLIGATED TO. THIS WILL BE OUR KARMA. IT IS NEVER TOO LATE TO IMPROVE ONE'S KARMA. WHAT GOES AROUND COMES AROUND. THIS IS EQUAL IN BOTH POSITIVE AND NEGATIVE ASPECTS. DO THINGS THAT ARE GENUINE AND FROM THE HEART, DO YOUR BEST TO MAINTAIN INTEGRITY, AND YOU WILL HAVE PEACE OF MIND. IT IS ALL UP TO YOU. LIVE THIS REALITY. YOUR LIFE IS IN YOUR OWN HANDS.

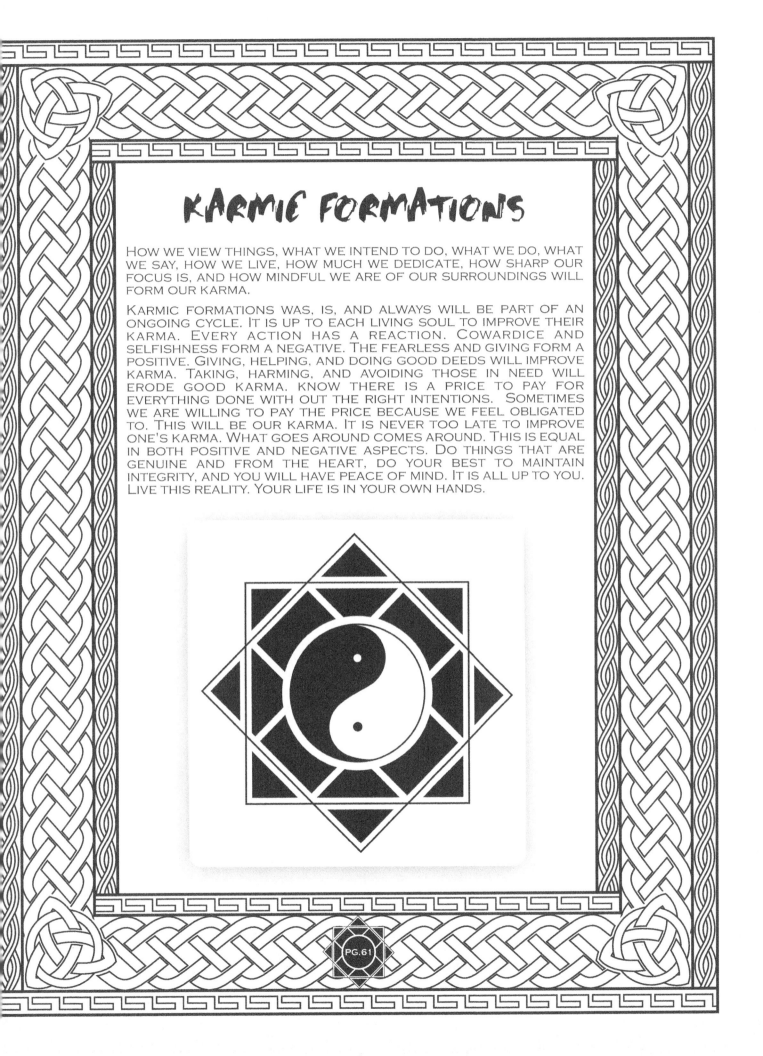

MINDFUL ACTIONS

BEING AWARE AND TAKING THE TIME TO STUDY AND ANALYZE EVERYTHING AROUND US, GIVES US A BETTER UNDERSTANDING OF HOW TO APPROACH EACH SITUATION. THIS COGNITION IS A SOLID FOUNDATION IN WHICH WE CAN USE TO MAKE OUR DECISIONS.

EVERYTHING WE SAY AND DO HAVE SOME TYPE OF EFFECT ON THOSE AROUND US. THEREFORE WE MUST BE THOUGHTFUL AND CONSIDERATE WITH OUR WORDS AND ACTIONS.

OUR HUMBLE INTENTIONS, HOW WE GO ABOUT OUR DAILY CHALLENGES AND THE EFFORT WE PUT INTO OUR DAILY DUTIES IS A REFLECTION OF OUR MIND SET. HAVING A CLEAR FOCUSED MIND WILL ACHIEVE THE BEST RESULTS.

BY BEING PATIENT AND ATTENTIVE WE SEE THINGS MUCH MORE CLEARLY. THIS REALIZATION GUIDES US TO BE CALM WITH OUT OVERREACTING. A FORCE OF NONRESISTANCE CAN ADMINISTER A PEACEFUL OUTCOME. THIS BRINGS AWARENESS TO A PERSON'S THOUGHTS AND INTENTIONS. AN ATTITUDE FREE OF FEAR AND AGGRESSION BRINGS EVERYTHING TO LIGHT.

BEING IN TUNED TO ALL ASPECTS OF OUR LIFE CAN BE REWARDING. WE CAN CULTIVATE OUR MIND AND BODY TO WORK TOGETHER IN HARMONY. WITH THOSE WE CARE ABOUT WE CAN SEE WHAT MAKES THEM HAPPY. WE WILL ALSO BE ABLE TO DETECT ANYTHING THAT IS HURTFUL OR CAUSES SADNESS. THIS HELPS US CREATE A BETTER ENVIRONMENT TO LIVE IN.

AT WORK WE REALIZE THE MOST PRODUCTIVE WAY TO REFORM OUR TASKS, ALL THE WHILE ENJOYING WHAT WE DO. OUR BIGGEST GOALS CAN BE WITHIN OUR REACH. WE MAY FIND A CAUSE WE BELIEVE IN. ALL THESE ATTRIBUTES GIVES US PEACE OF MIND.

OUR PRINCIPLES, BELIEFS, AND OUTLOOK GUIDE OUR LIFE. IN A RETICENT STATE WE TEND TO BE MORE MINDFUL OF THE WORLD AROUND US. THE FREEDOM OF OUR MINDS IS VAST. WHEN WE RELAX AND CONCENTRATE WE CAN SEE EVERYTHING WITH HUMILITY.

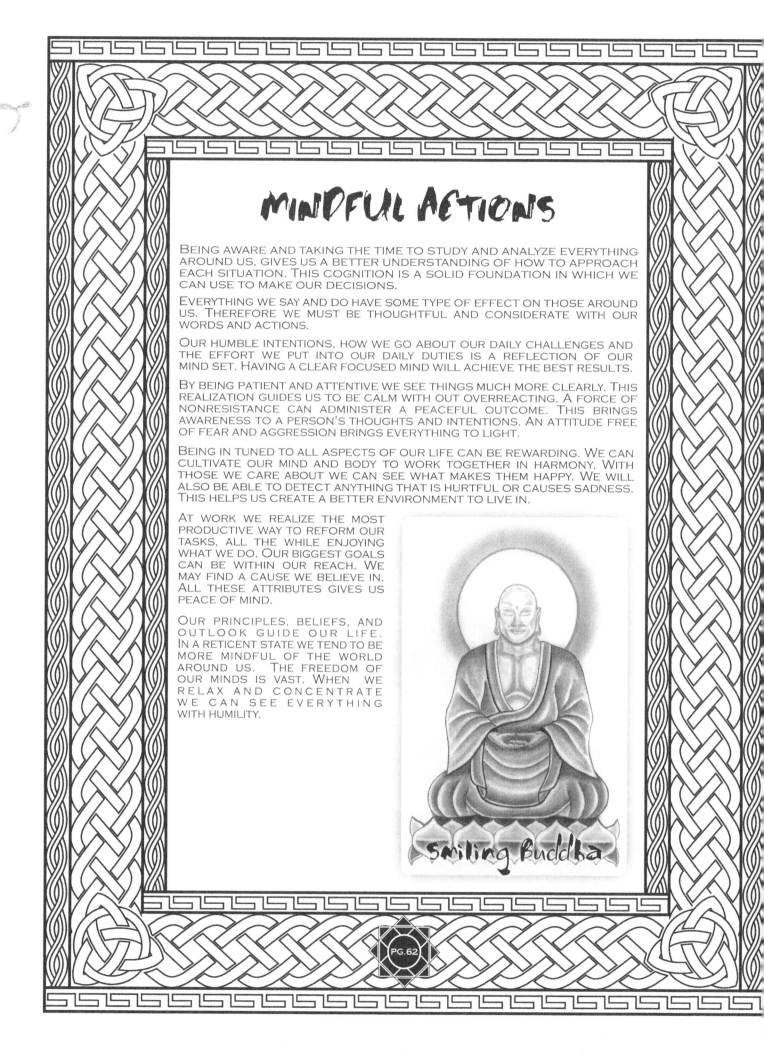

Smiling Buddha

IN THE NAME OF LOVE

LOVE IS THE ONE THING THAT MAKES OUR LIVES FEEL COMPLETE. LOVING OUR FAMILY, OUR OCCUPATION, AND OUR HOUSEHOLD GIVES US A HARMONIC SENSE OF BALANCE. THIS BALANCE ALLOWS OUR HOPES AND DREAMS TO BARE FRUIT AND BRING HAPPINESS INTO OUR LIVES.

AS WE GROW OUR PARENTS LOVE HELPS GUIDE US TO SEE EVERYTHING THAT'S AVAILABLE IN LIFE. AS WE GET OLDER WE MEET AND LEARN FROM ALL TYPES OF PEOPLE. ALONG THIS ROAD WE LEARN WHAT WE TRULY DESIRE. WE BECOME AWARE OF OUR MINDFUL SEARCH FOR AN EXTENSION OF OURSELVES. SOME OF US FIND SOUL MATES. FRIENDS FIRST, THEN LOVERS. THIS TYPE OF ROMANCE IS A CONSTANTLY BURNING FLAME OF COMPASSION AND UNDERSTANDING WITH A UNIQUE FORM OF LOYALTY. TOGETHER MANY THINGS ARE EXPERIENCED WHICH INCLUDE PASSION, CONFLICT, AND EVEN TRAGEDY. IN EACH OTHERS ARMS, LOVE AND SUPPORT FOR ONE ANOTHER CAN OVERCOME ANYTHING. MAKING LOVE BECOMES A POWERFUL UNION BETWEEN TWO SOULS BEING BOTH PASSIONATE AND SACRED. GETTING MARRIED AND BEING BLESSED WITH CHILDREN PROVIDES US WITH A SENSE OF ACCOMPLISHMENT. AS OUR CHILDREN GROW WE EXPERIENCE A NEW FOUND JOY. OUR LOVE GUIDES THEM JUST LIKE OUR PARENTS DID FOR US WHEN WE WERE CHILDREN.

ALONG THE PATH OF LIFE WE GAIN MANY FRIENDS. SOME BONDS STARTED EARLY IN OUR LIVES, HAVING WITHSTOOD THE TEST OF TIME AND STILL THRIVING TODAY. THESE BONDS FILL US WITH PRIDE. WE FEEL A WARM LOVING SUPPORT FROM THESE INDIVIDUALS. THEY HAVE BECOME OUR BROTHERS AND SISTERS HAVING A PLACE IN OUR HEARTS. WHEN EVER WE NEED THEM THEY ARE THERE. THEY ARE IRREPLACEABLE.

A HAPPY HOME GIVES US A FEELING OF BOTH SATISFACTION AND CONTENTMENT. WE ARE VERY PROUD OF ANY IMPROVEMENTS TO OUR HOMES. ALL SPECIAL OCCASIONS ARE FILLED WITH LAUGHTER AND JOY. THESE ARE WONDERFUL TIMES WITH HAPPY THOUGHTS RUNNING WILD. THIS ATMOSPHERE IS A GREAT FOUNDATION TO FUEL FURTHER SUCCESS IN OUR LIVES.

ENJOYING WHAT WE DO FOR A LIVING IS A POSITIVE REFLECTION OF WHO WE ARE. WHEN WE LOVE WHAT WE DO WE ARE BLESSED BECAUSE EVERYTHING MAKES PERFECT SENSE. THIS GIVES OUR LIFE MEANING AND PURPOSE. WITH A POSITIVE OUTLOOK IT IS EASY TO LOVE AND APPRECIATE EVERYTHING WE DO. IT IS OUR PRINCIPLES THAT TAKE US DOWN THIS ROAD WITH A CONTINUOUS FLOW.

WE FEEL A STRONG SENSE OF GRATITUDE TO BE ABLE TO SHARE OUR THOUGHTS AND FEELINGS WITH THOSE WE HOLD DEAR. EACH DAY OUR APPRECIATION AND HUMILITY INSPIRE US TO MAKE THE MOST OF EVERYTHING. ALL THIS BEING ACHIEVED IN THE NAME OF LOVE.

Guan Yin

A COMPASSIONATE WORLD

SOMETIMES WHETHER WE LIKE IT OR NOT WE ARE AFFECTED BY THE CIRCUMSTANCES OF OTHERS. IT IS ALMOST AS IF WE CAN HEAR AND FEEL THEIR NEEDS. WE PUT OURSELVES IN THEIR SHOES AND WE FEEL SADNESS. THESE FEELINGS CANNOT BE IGNORED.

WHEN WE WITNESS PEOPLE INFECTED WITH MISERY IT MANIFESTS AN UNEASINESS WITHIN US. WHEN IT'S A CLOSE FRIEND WE OFFER OUR HEART. WHEN SOMEONE IS LESS FORTUNATE WE WILL GIVE FOOD OR MONEY. WE WISH WE COULD SNAP OUR FINGERS AND FIX ALL THEIR PROBLEMS. IN SITUATIONS OF UNCERTAINTY INSPIRING HOPE AND CONFIDENCE FEELS LIKE THE LEAST WE CAN DO.

SOMETIMES THE ROLE IS REVERSED. WHEN WE SUFFER A LOSS, WE FEEL ANXIETY AND EMPTINESS. WE MAY ALSO FEEL DISHEARTENED FROM A FAILURE OR SETBACK. IN THESE TIMES OF NEED HAVING SOMEONE TO SHARE DIALOGUE WITH HELPS US DEAL WITH OUR CRISIS. OUR FRIENDS AND FAMILY MAY NOT BE AVAILABLE. WE FEEL DISAPPOINTMENT BELIEVING THEY HAVE THEIR OWN LIVES TO LIVE AND DON'T CARE ABOUT US. WE FEEL, TO THEM, WE ARE OUT OF SIGHT OUT OF MIND. WE APPRECIATE THE SMALLEST GESTURES BECAUSE IT LETS US KNOW PEOPLE STILL THINK ABOUT US. WHEN WE KNOW OUR FRIENDS CARE ABOUT OUR WELL-BEING IN MAKES US FEEL GREAT.

IN SOME CASES THERE IS NOT MUCH THAT CAN BE DONE TO FIX THE PHYSICAL ASPECT OF A SITUATION. WE TRY TO HELP THOSE IN NEED TO BECOME STRONG AND OFFER THEM WORDS OF ENCOURAGEMENT. WE LET THEM KNOW THAT THEY ARE NOT ALONE AND WE WILL DO WHATEVER WE CAN TO HELP. DURING THIS PROCESS WE TRY TO HELP THEM UNDERSTAND THE POSITIVE SIDE OF THINGS. THIS ENABLES THEM TO SEE ALL OF THE GOOD THINGS THAT ARE AVAILABLE TO THEM. ONCE THEY REALIZE THIS THEY CAN ELIMINATE THE MENTAL POISONING AND BECOME HAPPIER PEOPLE. THEY CAN USE THE PRESENT TO CORRECT THE PAST, WHICH IN TURN WILL IMPROVE THE FUTURE. A BETTER UNDERSTANDING PRESENTS A MORE FAVOURABLE VIEW. BEING THERE FOR PEOPLE IN TIMES OF NEED MAKES US FEEL PERSONAL MERIT. WHEN OUR COMPASSION HELPS THEM BECOME STRONGER AND GET OVER THEIR NOT SO GOOD CIRCUMSTANCES, WE FEEL CONTENT. WHEN PEOPLE CARE ABOUT ONE ANOTHER THE WORLD IS A BETTER PLACE.

George Washington

FREEDOM FROM OPPRESSION

WE DON'T KNOW HOW LUCKY WE ARE UNTIL OUR RIGHTS AND LIBERTY ARE RESTRICTED. HAVING A CHOICE, WHAT WE THINK AND EXPRESS BECOME OUTLETS OF INDEPENDENCE. GOVERNMENT COMES IN MANY FORMS, ALL BEING EVENTUAL OPPRESSORS. OVER TIME WE ARE WEIGHED DOWN AS OUR SUPPOSED FREEDOMS CONTINUALLY BECOME SMALLER AND SMALLER. AS GOVERNMENTS GET AWAY WITH THE UNTHINKABLE THEY BECOME MORE BOLD. THEIR ABUSE OF POWER IS RAMPANT. WHAT WAS ONCE CONSIDERED AN OUTRAGE IS NOW ACCEPTABLE. COMMUNISM, SOCIALISM, AND A DEMOCRATIC REPUBLIC ALL END UP BEING ONE OF THE SAME. THESE TERMS ARE MERELY A LABEL OF DISGUISE. A GOVERNMENT BY THE PEOPLE, FOR THE PEOPLE, BECOMES A DREAM FROM THE PAST. ALL THE WHILE THE VAST MAJORITY OF THE UPPER CLASS CONSPIRE TO DICTATE TO THE MIDDLE AND LOWER CLASS.

AS THIS HAPPENS PEOPLE REALIZE OUR FREEDOM IS REALLY A CAREFULLY PLANNED ILLUSION. IT TAKES A MAN OF POWER TO STAND UP FOR WHAT'S RIGHT NO MATTER WHAT THE ODDS. THE PEOPLE WILL SUPPORT THIS TYPE OF INDIVIDUAL. THE GREAT LEADER AND RIGHTEOUS REVOLUTIONARY GEORGE WASHINGTON WAS THIS TYPE OF MAN. HE FOUGHT FOR FREEDOM FROM OPPRESSORS, WHICH IN HIS CASE WAS THE BRITISH. HE PUT EVERYTHING ON THE LINE AND BELIEVED IN THE CAUSE WHOLEHEARTEDLY. WHEN HE EMERGED THE VICTOR HE FULFILLED HIS GOAL AND PLEDGED A GOVERNMENT, BY THE PEOPLE, FOR THE PEOPLE. A CONSTITUTION WAS SET TO BACK UP THESE DREAMS OF GRANDEUR. IT WAS ONCE SAID THAT THEY WOULD RATHER LET 200 GUILTY MEN GO FREE THAN IMPRISON ONE INNOCENT MAN. TODAY THAT NO LONGER APPLIES. CENTURIES LATER POLITICAL CORRUPTION WITH NOBLE SELF INTERESTS HAVE PUT LIMITS ON OUR LIBERTY. LIES AND MANIPULATION ARE THE SOURCE OF THEIR PERSUASION. NOT EVERYONE HAS TURNED A BLIND EYE BUT FEW CAN DO ANYTHING WITHOUT BEING THREATENED OR PUT IN PRISON.

WE NO LONGER HAVE MANY OPTIONS AS THE GOVERNMENT TIGHTENS ITS GRIP. BEING ABLE TO CHOOSE BETWEEN A POISONOUS SNAKE OR VENOMOUS SPIDER DOES NOT STOP US FROM BEING DEALT A DEADLY BLOW. WE ARE TOLD WHAT WE CAN AND CANNOT DO AND IF WE DO NOT OBLIGE WE ARE SEVERELY PUNISHED WITHOUT ANY COMPASSION OR MERCY. NO ONE REALIZES THIS UNTIL THEY'RE IN THE GOVERNMENT'S GRASP. THERE IS PLENTY OF PROOF WITHIN THE PRISON SYSTEM. WITH 1 OUT OF 31 AMERICANS IN PRISON OR ON SUPERVISED RELEASE NOT MUCH MORE NEEDS TO BE SAID. ALCOHOL AND CIGARETTES ARE LEGAL, YET THEY CAUSE ADDICTION, SUFFERING AND DEATH. THEIR AFFECTS ARE NO DIFFERENT THAN THE DRUGS THAT WERE SOLD BY A MAN THAT IS NOW SERVING A LIFE SENTENCE FOR A NON-VIOLENT OFFENSE. OUR SOCIETY HAS BECOME AN HYPOCRISY NOT A DEMOCRACY. MEDIA HYPE AND EMOTION ARE NOT SUPPOSED TO SENTENCE PEOPLE, BUT, MORE OFTEN THEN NOT THEY DO.

THERE IS NO LONGER CLARITY AS TO WHO ARE THE GOOD GUYS AND THE BAD ONES. LINES HAVE BEEN CROSSED, CONDITIONS HAVE BEEN FABRICATED AND STANDARDS HAVE BEEN CHANGED. FEDERAL PROSECUTORS HAVE A 97% CONVICTION RATE GETTING BONUSES FROM THE HARSHEST PUNISHMENTS BEING DEALT. IF DEALS ARE NOT STUCK BEFORE THE TRIAL THE RETRIBUTION IS EXTREME. MANY QUESTIONS WITH NOT ENOUGH ANSWERS. WHEN IS ENOUGH, ENOUGH?

ONLY WHEN THE PEOPLE STAND TOGETHER CAN THEIR VOICES BE HEARD. WHEN EVERYONE STOPS TURNING THE OTHER CHEEK AND INSTEAD RAISE THEIR HANDS UP, THE ABUSE WILL STOP. BEING DIVIDED AND DOCILE HAS ALLOWED THIS TREACHERY TO TAKE PLACE. WHEN EVERYONE FEELS THE SAME WAY AND ARE UNITED IN THEIR BELIEFS THE POWER CAN ONCE AGAIN GO TO THE PEOPLE. FREEDOM HAS NO BIAS AND IS FOR EVERYONE TO ENJOY.

THE BALANCE OF POWER

In this world Earth, wind, fire and water can give life or cause destruction. Together these elements form the ultimate energy. Within the Earth there are mountains, metals, and vegetation. Wind gives the breath of life and can influence other elements. The sun, friction or volcanoes can create fire. Without fire there is no warmth. Water is the most diverse of all the elements. Water has the ability to penetrate any solid substance, it can also stop fire. Water is part of every living creation and prolongs life.

Human nature can be compared to the best and worst aspects of Earth, wind, fire and water. Stability and confidence makes one think of the earth. The unrelenting force that creates strength and speed represents the wind. Comfort or anger can be a characteristic caused by fire. Water can destroy or create peace and harmony. Power can be used to do good deeds. Just as it can spawn evil. Some will give, some will take. Some will be fair, some will abuse. When a man craves power, he is the type that will never maintain it. When a man doesn't crave power, his personal integrity will be tested. A decent man can be manipulated and give into temptation. Which will forever change the course of his life. A calm rational man will achieve the best results. Selfishness, ambition and conceit will assure failure and grant a horrible fate. An honest, humble, grateful man will prevail in an everlasting fashion. Beware of the envious man who craves power. His thirst will cause division and destruction. The man with money and wealth that uses it to control people and countries, owns bad karma more than anything else. See power for what it is. This realm must find a balance otherwise there will be nothing but chaos and destruction. May all the righteous men of integrity prevail.

THOUGHTS THAT PERSEVERE

I BELIEVE IN HAVING A STRONG FAMILY THAT WILL HELP, GUIDE AND ENCOURAGE EACH OTHER THROUGH THE GOOD TIMES AND THE BAD.

I BELIEVE THAT SMILING IN THE FACE OF FEAR TO HONOR THOSE WHO YOU CARE ABOUT IS BEING LOYAL AND TRUE.

I BELIEVE IN INTEGRITY, RIGHTEOUSNESS, AND LETTING YOUR ACTIONS SPEAK FOR THEMSELVES.

I BELIEVE IN CONTINUAL IMPROVEMENT, HAVING A POSITIVE ATTITUDE, ENJOYING LIFE, AND ACHIEVING GOALS. I BELIEVE THAT A WINNING ATTITUDE IS CONTAGIOUS. IF YOU ARE SURROUNDED BY SUCCESSFUL CONFIDENT PEOPLE YOU WILL PROSPER.

I BELIEVE THAT STRONG MINDS POSSESS AN INDOMITABLE SPIRIT THAT WILL NEVER GIVE UP OR SURRENDER.

I BELIEVE IN HAVING A FIGHTING SPIRIT AND STANDING UP FOR WHAT YOU BELIEVE IN. NOT EVERY BATTLE CAN BE WON BUT KNOWLEDGE, EXPERIENCE, AND PATIENCE WILL WIN THE WAR.

I BELIEVE IN MAKING THE BEST OF EVERY SITUATION AND NEVER GIVING UP HOPE FOR A MORE POSITIVE ONE. THE WORLD IS CONSTANTLY CHANGING NO CIRCUMSTANCE WILL ALWAYS REMAIN THE SAME.

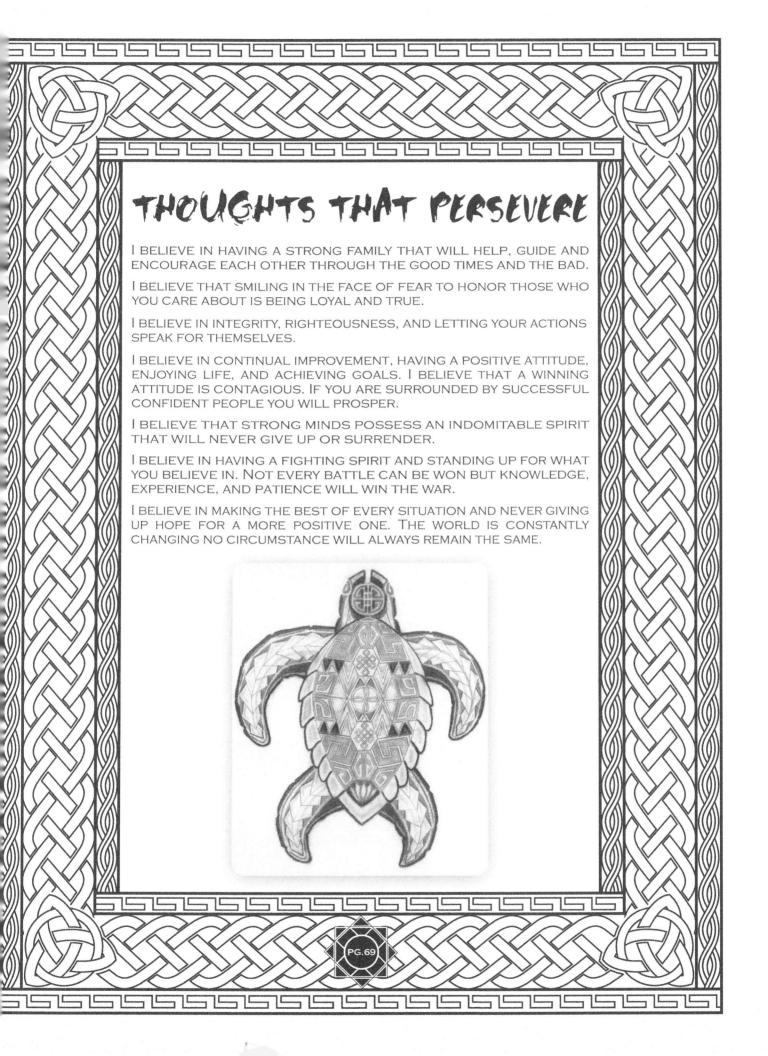

EPILOGUE

We hope you, the reader, found something of value within this text. Any gain made is great.

As this book comes to an end, we have included some of the author's thoughts at different intervals, which all helped establish the road toward the creation of this book. Some of these works are unrestrained and bold. There are 6 writings in total. They include "A Cowards Karma" ; which is the author's true feelings on the subject. "Action Speaks Louder Than Words" is designed to expose people that harbor bad intentions. "In Freedom We Trust" shows how things have become, but still inspires hope when our freedom is jeopardized by a corrupt system. "Down But Not Out" was written at a time when the author was experiencing horrendous treatment thanks to the requests of Federal Prosecutors. "Never Say Never" is an attitude that persistence will always pay off. "Crowned Kings" is a victory dance which seemed like the best way to end this book. We wish the readers of this book lots of luck and prosperity. It is with our best intentions that these words add incite into your arsenal of life. May all real men prevail.

A COWARDS KARMA

WHAT A PERSON THINKS, SAYS AND DOES REFLECTS THEIR KARMA. A PERSON WITH A GOOD HEART AND MIND IS INVALUABLE. SOME PEOPLE WALK PATHS THAT ARE HONEST AND TRUE. OTHERS TRY TO FABRICATE THEIR EXISTENCE TO HIDE THEIR SHAME. A PERSON IN A TIME OF NEED WILL FIND OUT WHO THEIR FRIENDS ARE. PASSIONATE CARING PEOPLE ARE THE KIND YOU CAN COUNT ON. KNOW THE PEOPLE THAT ONLY SHOW THEIR FACES WHEN THEY HAVE SOMETHING TO GAIN. DEEP DOWN THEY HATE AND ARE ONLY THERE TO TAKE. INFECTIOUS PEOPLE BRING BAD LUCK. THEY MUST BE AVOIDED THEY WILL DRAIN YOU AND EVENTUALLY DESTROY YOUR SUCCESS. A REAL MAN'S ACTIONS SPEAK WITH HONOR BECAUSE HE HAS THE RIGHT INTENTIONS. THE SELF MOTIVATED MAN ALWAYS HAS SOMETHING TO HIDE HE LIVES A LIFE OF LIES. HIS DISHONESTY TRAILS HIM. REAL MEN ARE COMMITTED TO THEIR BELIEFS AND THEY WOULD RATHER DIE THAN BETRAY THEM. HEAVEN HAS NO LOVE FOR A COWARD, THAT'S WHY THEIR LIVE'S ARE A LIVING HELL. A PERSON'S ACTIONS FORM THEIR KARMA, THEIR INTENTIONS ARE THE BODY OF THEIR SOUL. SELFISH COWARDS ARE CURSED AND THEIR INSECURITIES THRIVE. MEN OF VALOUR OVERCOME AND ADAPT TO ANY SITUATION BECAUSE THEY ARE TRIED, TESTED AND TRUE.

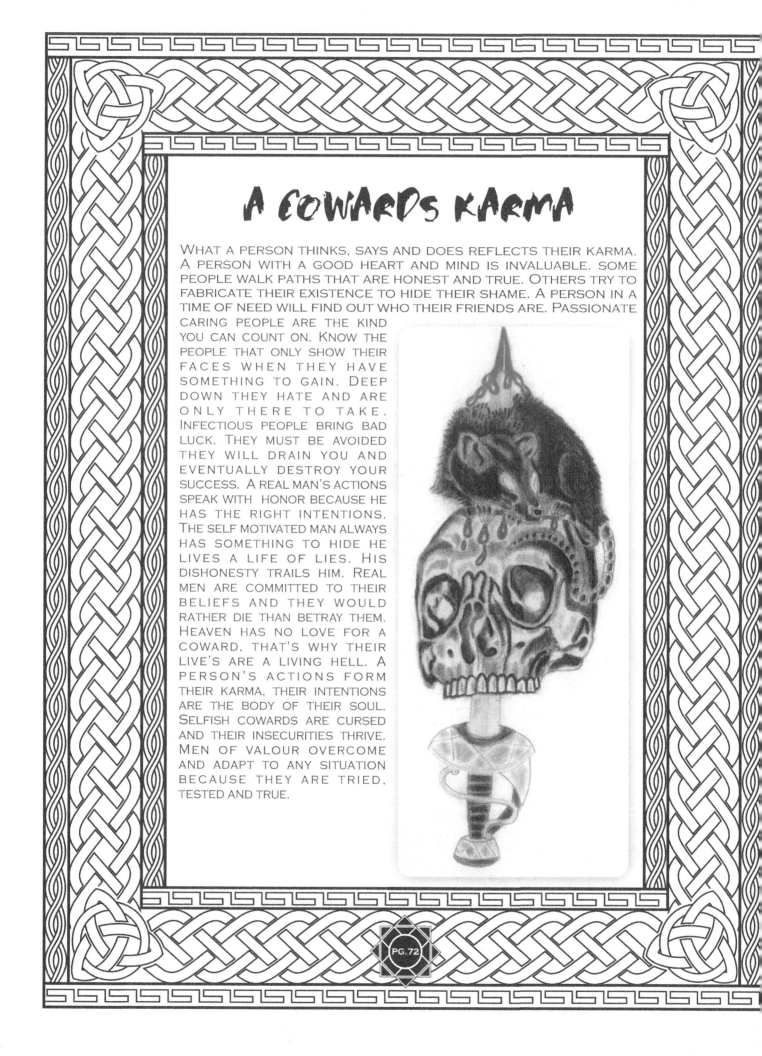

ACTIONS SPEAK LOUDER THAN WORDS

SUCCESSFUL PEOPLE WORK HARD TO ACHIEVE THEIR GOALS AND ESTABLISH THEIR REPUTATIONS. WHAT THEY SAY AND DO SPEAKS FOR ITSELF.

HATERS AND SELFISH PEOPLE ARE ONE OF THE SAME. THEY ARE SELF-SERVING ALWAYS TALKING ABOUT ME, MYSELF, AND I.

JEALOUS, INSECURE, AND UNSUCCESSFUL THEIR LIVES ARE FULL OF BITTERNESS AND ENVY. THEY WILL DISCREDIT SOMEONE ELSE'S SUCCESS, TRY TO TARNISH A PERSON'S REPUTATION AND BELITTLE OTHERS IN AN ATTEMPT TO ELEVATE THEIR OWN STATUS.

THEY PREFER THE COMPANY OF FOLLOWERS AND HARBOR A GRUDGE TOWARDS PEOPLE WHO HAVE WITNESSED THEIR SHORTCOMINGS. BEING UNDERACHIEVERS MAKES THEM DECEITFUL. THEY TAKE CREDIT FOR THE SUCCESS OF OTHERS AND ALWAYS WANT WHAT THEY CAN'T HAVE.

IT'S NOT HARD TO BE HONEST AND TRUE. BE REAL, DON'T HATE. ACTIONS SPEAK LOUDER THAN WORDS. LIFE IS TOO SHORT TO ENVY OTHER PEOPLES SUCCESS, CELEBRATE YOUR OWN.

IN FREEDOM WE TRUST

They want to break you, dictate your fate put you in a dark place, make you feel useless and alone, take away your phone. They want you consumed with worry and fear, make your fighting spirit disappear. The government's system is used when other rules don't permit. Hearsay and snitches on the stand bear witness. They make rules as they choose so whatever battle with them you will lose. Family and friends around you will suffer. They play dirty never fair, they want you on your knees to beg and plead in despair. They have amazing hate. They want you to be a quivering selfish coward. Take your soul. It makes them feel in control. It would be a miracle to be treated fair, but it's a chance we don't have a choice to make. In freedom we trust. To win this war it's a must. In life all real men get put to the test, before they get laid to rest. Don't give up, it's never too late. Fighting for freedom is a worthy fate.

DOWN BUT NOT OUT

IN A LAND WHERE THE LAW HAS HATE AND THEY GO OUT OF THEIR WAY TO MAKE YOU FEEL PAIN. THEY LAUGH WHEN THEY SEE YOU SUFFER, THEY DON'T CARE ABOUT THE PAIN OF YOUR SIGNIFICANT OTHERS THEY DON'T CARE WHAT YOU DO OR SAY, THE SELF RIGHTEOUS BASTARDS FABRICATE AND MANIPULATE TO GET THEIR WAY. WITH CHAINS ON MY ANKLES AND WRISTS, THEY KNOW THEY CAN'T BREAK ME, SO THEY SAY I'M A SECURITY RISK. THEIR BULLETS CAN'T KILL ME, I WON'T LET THEM DEFEAT ME, EVEN WITH MY HEART BLEEDING, I WON'T BE RETREATING. I MIGHT BE DOWN BUT I'M NOT OUT, I WILL KEEP MOVING FORWARD AND MAKE EVERYONE PROUD.

- MARCH 5, 2009 THE DAY THEY PUT THE AUTHOR ON A THREE MAN HOLD.

Archangel samuel

NEVER SAY NEVER

WHEN YOU WANT SOMETHING GO AND GET IT. BE LIKE WATER, DON'T LET ANYTHING STAND IN YOUR WAY. KNOWLEDGE IS POWER, PRACTICE MAKES PERFECT, BE PATIENT AND PERSEVERE. DON'T LET THE SITUATION DISHEARTEN YOU, THINGS ARE NOT ALWAYS WHAT THEY SEEM, WHERE THERE IS A WILL, THERE IS A WAY. NEVER SAY NEVER, STOP AT NOTHING TO ACHIEVE WHAT YOU DESIRE. PERSISTENCE ALWAYS PAYS OFF, LET THE BLOOD PUMP THROUGH YOUR VEINS WITH ONE GOAL IN MIND.

CROWNED KINGS

THEIR DESTINY IS DEFINED WITH A KINGDOM IN MIND. BORN TO REIGN SUPREME AND REACH GREAT HEIGHTS. THEIR FIGHTING SPIRITS THRIVE. THEY ARE ELITE WARRIORS READY FOR A TRIUMPHANT MOMENT OF GLORY. ALL CHALLENGES ARE EMBRACED WITH WAR PAINT ON THEIR FACE. WHEN THE MOMENT ARRIVES, THEY SCREAM LOUD WAR CRIES. ONCE THEY UNLEASH THE WRATH, THERE'S NO LOOKING BACK. ATTACKS DEPLOYED, VICTORY IS BOUND, RIVALS DESTROYED, THE KINGS SHALL BE CROWNED.

ABOUT THE AUTHOR

CLAY ROUECHE IS FROM VANCOUVER B.C . AN ARTIST , A PHILOSOPHER , A POET , AND NOW AN AUTHOR. OFTEN CALLED WORLDLY AND CHARISMATIC , CLAY'S KNOWLEDGE AND WISDOM HAS COME FROM HIS MANY LIFE EXPERIENCES. HE INHERITED HIS MILITARY MIND SET. ONE OF HIS GREAT GRANDFATHERS WAS A US NAVY MIDDLE WEIGHT BOXING CHAMPION AND HIS GRANDFATHER WAS A MASTER MASON WHO RECEIVED THE MEDAL OF HONOR WHILE SERVING IN THE CANADIAN AIR FORCE DURING WORLD WAR II. CLAY ALSO HAS A PASSION FOR MARTIAL ARTS AND IS A VERY DISCIPLINED INDIVIDUAL. FURTHERMORE HE HAS A WAY WITH WORDS. WHILE ATTENDING SOME SALES TRAINING FRESH OUT OF HIGHSCHOOL IT BECAME VERY CLEAR THAT HE HAD NATURAL COMMUNICATION SKILLS.

CLAY HAS ALWAYS HAD A LOVE OF HISTORY. GROWING UP IN A COMMUNITY FULL OF IMMIGRANTS ALLOWED HIM TO EXPERIENCE MANY DIFFERENT CUSTOMS FIRST HAND. LATER HE TRAVELLED ALL OVER THE WORLD TO PLACES LIKE EUROPE , LATIN AMERICA , THE MIDDLE EAST , AND ASIA. DURING HIS WORLDLY TRAVELS HE ACQUIRED KNOWLEDGE FROM MANY DIFFERENT TYPES OF PEOPLE , MANY OF WHOM BECAME HIS LIFE LONG FRIENDS. HAVING A NATURAL GIFT HE WAS OPENLY ACCEPTED AS AN EQUAL INTO MANY DIFFERENT CULTURES. CLAY TRULY HAS LIVED AND EXPERIENCED THINGS MOST PEOPLE COULDN'T EVEN FATHOM. HE LIVED HIS DREAM.

THIS ALL CAME AT A PRICE. ON MAY 17 2008 HE WAS ARRESTED WHILE TRAVELLING ON VACATION TO MEXICO. THERE WAS A JOINT OPERATION BETWEEN THE US , CANADA , AND MEXICO WHICH RESULTED IN HIS ARREST. HE WAS NOT GIVEN ANY EXTRADITION HEARING AND ARRIVED IN THE US BY MEANS OF EXTRAORDINARY RENDITION. ONCE IN US FEDERAL CUSTODY HE DEALT WITH THE HOSTILE TACTICS OF THE FEDERAL GOVERNMENT. MANY WOULD ARGUE THE TACTICS USED ON HIM WERE UNCONSTITUTIONAL. HIS PHONE PRIVILEGES WERE TAKEN AWAY AND HIS MAIL WAS DELAYED MONTHS AT A TIME.

CONTINUES ON NEXT PAGE

He was placed in a Special Housing Unit where he was locked down 23-24 hours a day in a small cell with bad lighting. When he was given his legal right to one hour recreation he was often called at 5am in the morning with his only option being to go out in the cold. He was locked down in this unit for almost two years ; this type of environment makes a lot of people lose their minds. It did not have that affect on Clay. Later Clay was given what's called "Diesel Therapy" taken early in the morning to an airport and flown around the US , not even his lawyer being notified about where he was going.

He eventually arrived in Marion , Illinois and was taken to a special Communication Management Unit that housed terrorists and Mob bosses. This Penitentiary was America's first Federal SuperMax prison. They did not break Clay. He stayed true to his belief's. Later due to excessive media attention and wide ranging US Federal Drug conspiracy Law's he had no choice but to accept an open plea in front of a Federal Judge where he was given 30 years. He said a few words , maintained his Dignity and took his sentence like a man.

Clay has been the subject of countless newspaper and magazine articles. Among the more popular stories are "The Last King of Potland" and more recently "BOSS WEED" in Rollingstones magazine. Clay is still actively pursued by all types of media. Not all of Clay's media attention has been negative. One former drug addict turned drug counselor did an interview with a newspaper and claimed Clay saved his life by helping him get clean. Currently many recovering drug addicts from all over North America write Clay letters of inspiration. He also gets letters from people with military backgrounds , some even being soldiers that have already been on tours of duty in Iraq and Afghanistan. Additionally Clay receives many letters of support from all types of people.

A natural born Entrepreneur with an unrelenting positive attitude Clay has continually turned all the negatives in his life to positives. This book is a classic example. A US prosecutor once said that Clay would of been very successful in anything he chose to do , but he had made the wrong choice. Now Clay has chosen to make the right choice and turn his life around. Some may see his situation as hopeless , but Clay has a much different view on things. Police on the street were quoted as saying Clay "Lived By a Code" and helped out his friends. Clay has always "Lived By a Code" and if he commits to something he will stop at nothing to live up to his obligations. A father and a family man first and foremost , Clay is loyal to his friends , and true to his roots. Because of the way Clay conducted himself all his friends and family support his decisions wholeheartedly. He is the type of man that will let his actions do the talking for him. It should be known that Clay is a realist , he knows he needs to reinvent himself and move his life in a more positive direction. And that is exactly what he plans to do.

All types of changes are being made with regards to the overcrowded US Federal prisons and the draconian drug laws. The system is broken and they are trying to fix it. With Marijuana slowly becoming legal all across the US and the War on Drugs coming to an end Clay might be able to go home to his family a lot sooner. He truly believes that which does not destroy us makes us stronger and that we can learn from our mistakes. Clay has turned over a new leaf and is all about improving his karma , which in turn will better his life.

Several Sources with in the media called Clay an anomaly , he is definitely not average or ordinary. His thoughts can't be contained ; his body may be in prison but his spirits running free. Clay truly is a renaissance man.

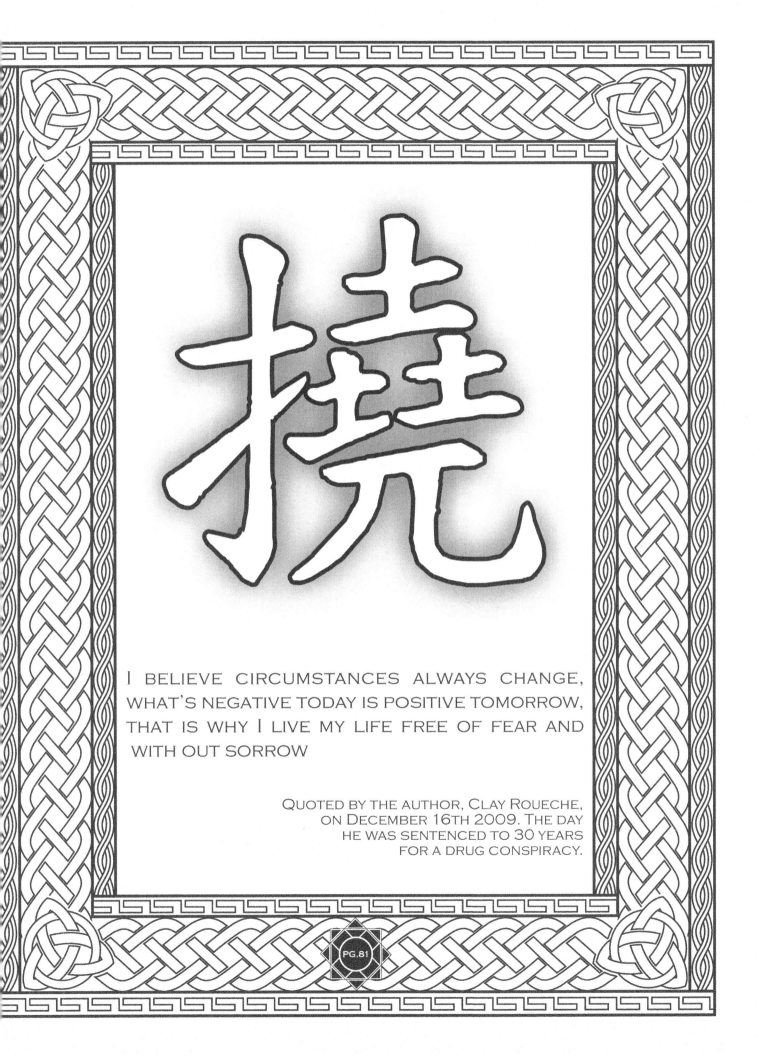

撬 圭

I BELIEVE CIRCUMSTANCES ALWAYS CHANGE,
WHAT'S NEGATIVE TODAY IS POSITIVE TOMORROW,
THAT IS WHY I LIVE MY LIFE FREE OF FEAR AND
 WITH OUT SORROW

QUOTED BY THE AUTHOR, CLAY ROUECHE,
ON DECEMBER 16TH 2009. THE DAY
HE WAS SENTENCED TO 30 YEARS
FOR A DRUG CONSPIRACY.

WWW.CLAYROUECHE.COM

Made in the USA
Monee, IL
14 June 2021